MW01625763

SAM GILLIAM

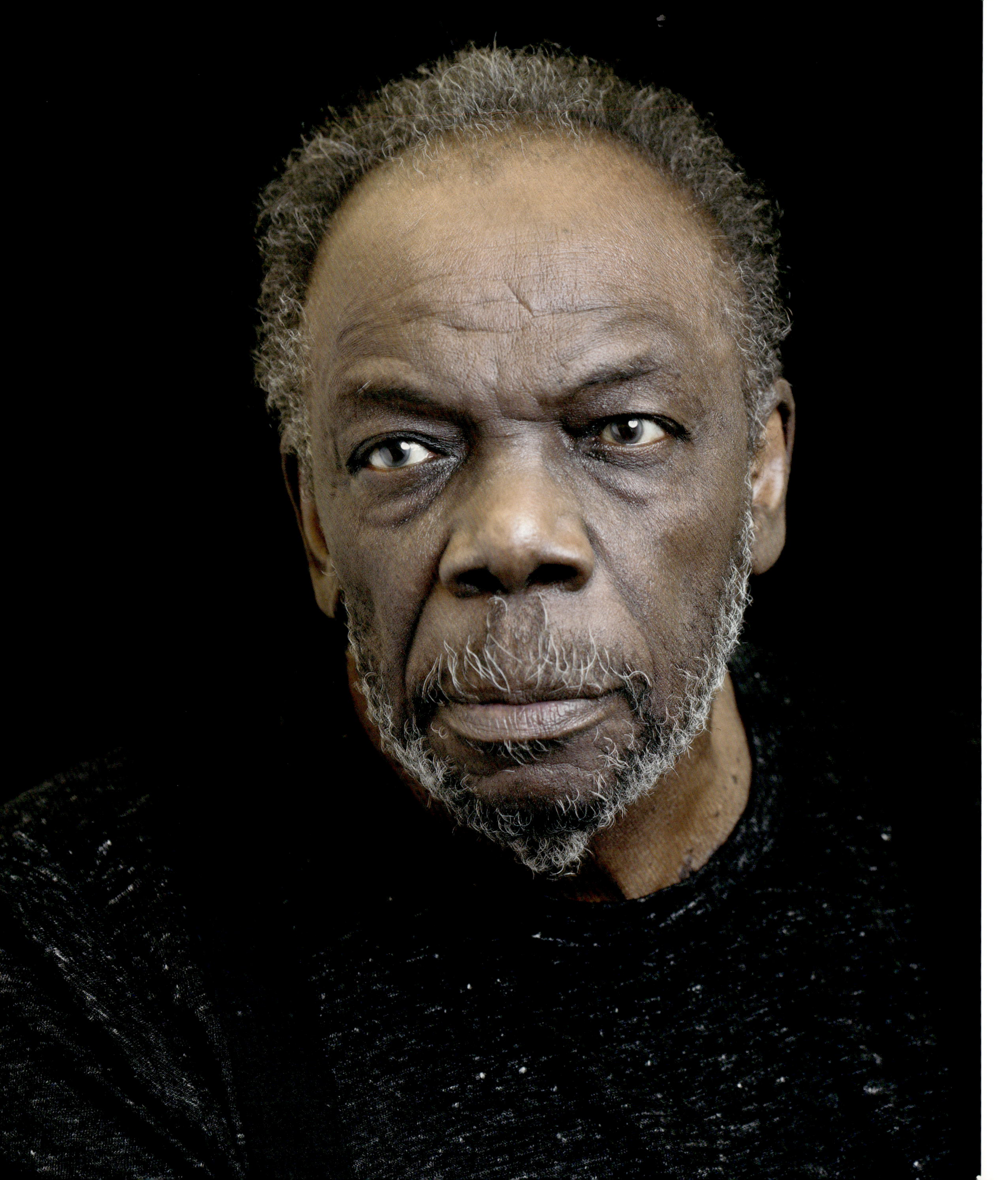

SAM GILLIAM

Existed Existing

510 & 540 West 25th Street, New York | November 6 – December 19, 2020

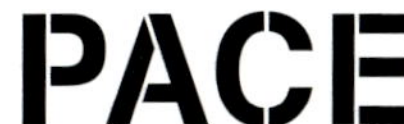

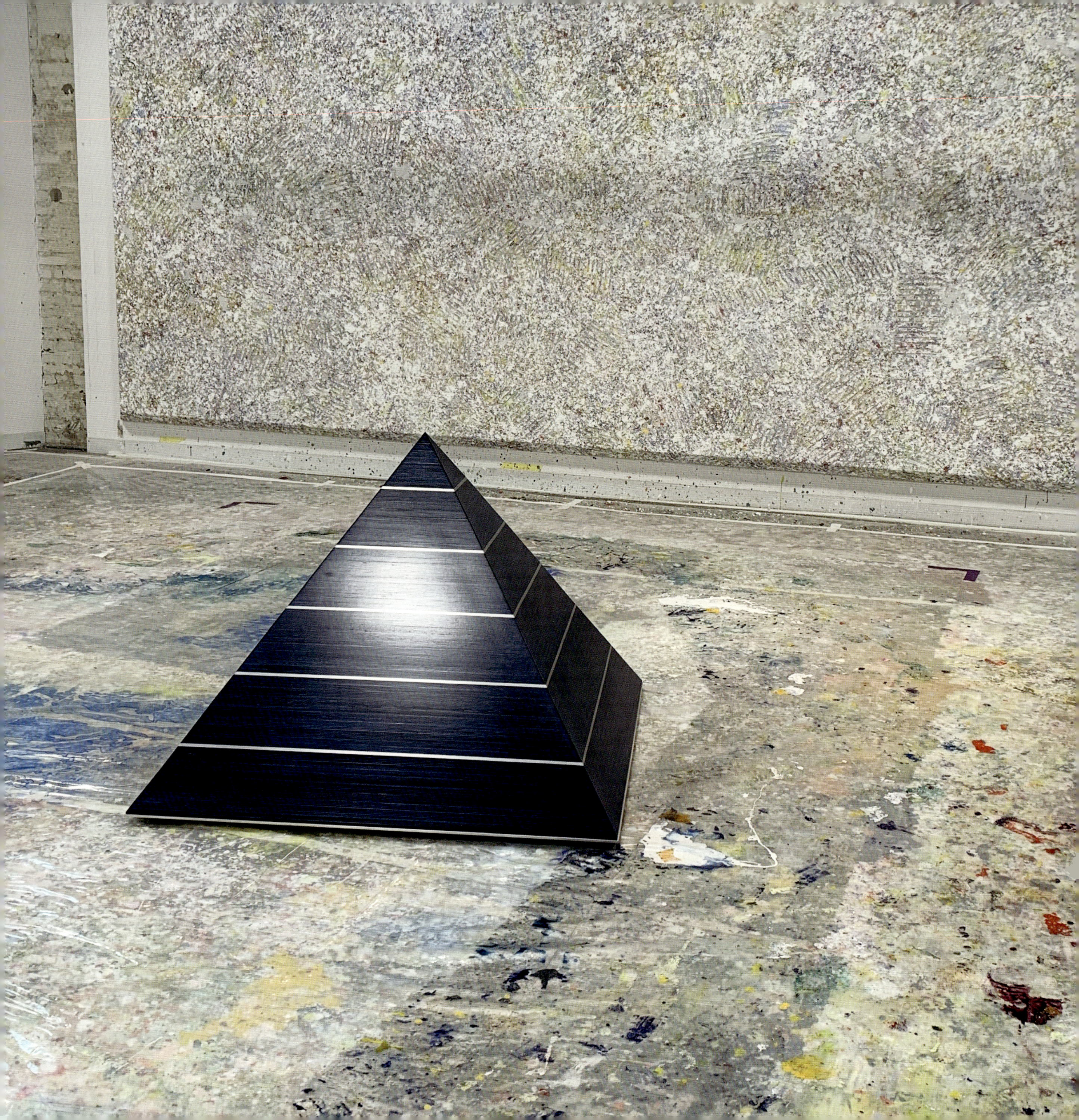

Sam Gilliam: In Process

Over the past three years, I made several visits to Sam Gilliam's studio in Washington DC, consulting with him in preparation for an exhibition of his new wood sculptures and works on paper. Made from stacked layers of plywood and thin sheets of aluminum, the sculptures are drenched in intense color, allowing the pattern of the wood grain to function as brushwork. As Sam has explained, their geometric forms are inspired by details from ancient Ethiopian architecture.

Concurrently, Sam produced a series of watercolors that he refers to as "Washi papers." Large, thick sheets of ripple-edged Japanese paper have been saturated with layer upon layer of monochromatic pigment, resembling skins or animal hides pinned up to dry. They appear to be made of color itself—red, blue, green, yellow, turquoise, cream, and white—and project real density, as opposed to the weightlessness of watercolor in the traditional sense of the medium. They harness color as a conduit for pure emotion. I am reminded of Agnes Martin talking to me about people's reticence toward abstraction: "From music, people accept pure emotion, but from art they demand explanation." Sam's sculptures and Washi papers defy explanation.

By January of 2020, our exhibition was set and three catalogue texts had been commissioned. Then the pandemic struck and sent us all into seclusion. Contact continued by phone and e-mail as we went on planning the exhibition. One day, about eight months ago, I received a communication from Annie Gawlak, Sam's wife, concerning details for framing the Washi papers. It ended with the cryptic words: "The boy is painting." More than once Sam had told me that he was finished with painting. But he is a painter and I was right not to believe him. By the time we were ready to exhibit the sculptures, the sorcerer's apprentice had assembled a flood of new work. Sam can't stop.

Annie sent me iPhone images of four new paintings in process. They appeared to be an extension of his stained canvas paintings of the '60s and '70s. More dynamic in their application and more intense in color, they were nevertheless clearly connected to the trajectory of his career. The exhibition and our plans for the installation would have to be reconsidered. The paintings deserved a gallery to themselves. With my curiosity piqued, I flew to Washington to see the new works as soon as they were stretched. When I arrived, gone were the color-field paintings I had expected and in their place, a series of predominately white paintings filled the studio: four of them eight-feet-by-eight feet and two eight-by-twenty feet. Monumental in scale, upon first glance these new works were vapors, appearing almost weightless. Yet on closer inspection, they were dense, crusty, and as heavy as volcanic ash with smoldering embers beneath.

Beginning with fields of color, Sam had layered the canvases with the history of his own development—ontogeny recapitulated phylogeny. Layers of paint materialized layers of ideas. Zooming past his white paintings of the 1970s, the slices, and his many works which free painting from the wall, these new canvases went further to incorporate physical materials from Sam's new sculptures. He retrieved the detritus from the construction of the sculptures—the sawdust and wood chips from the carpenter's floor—and mixed it with pigment, erupting in lavish surfaces that Sam clawed and raked to reveal bubbling color below. Now that this volcanic dust has settled, we are honored to present the results.

AG

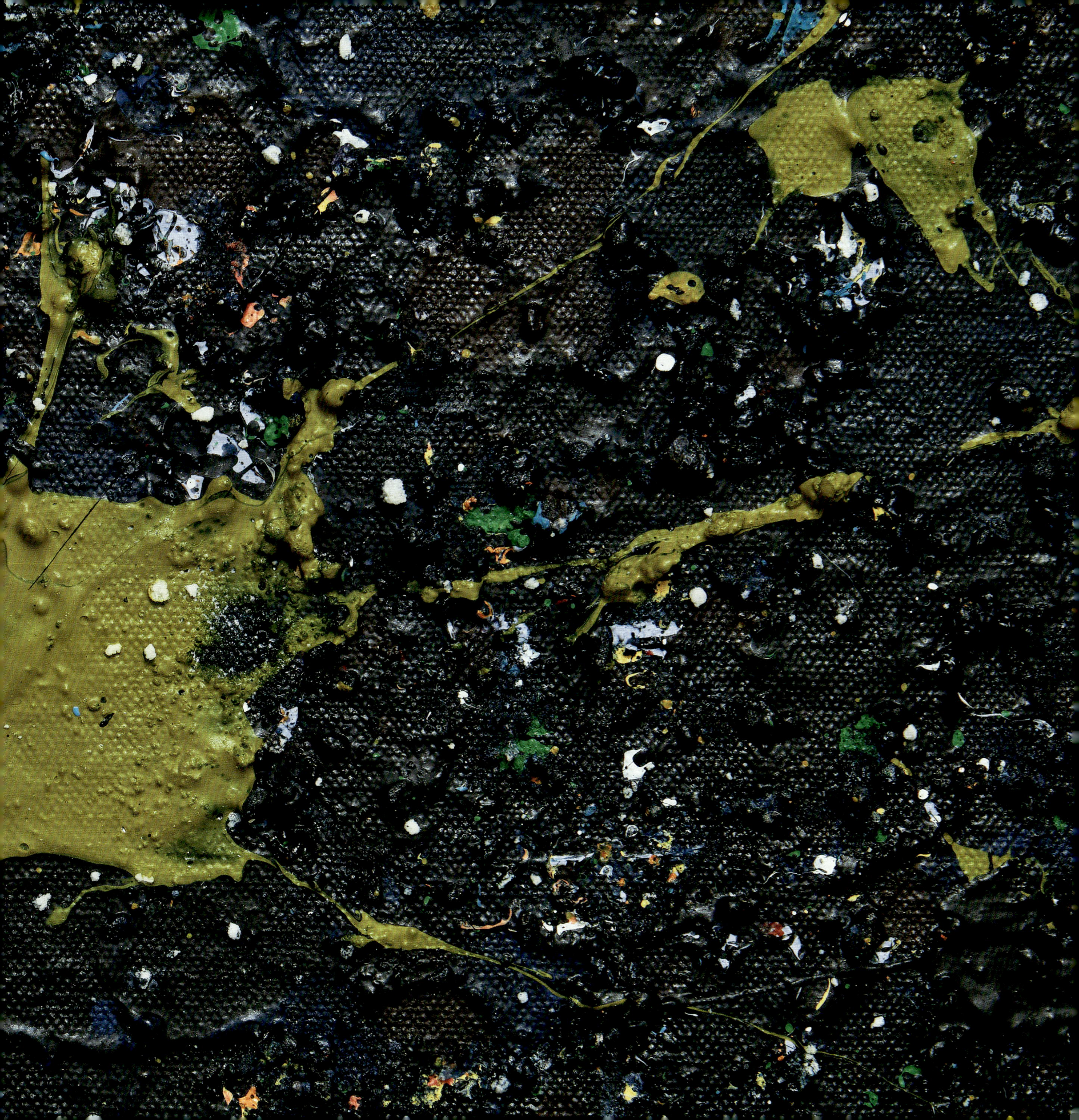

For John Lewis | 2020 | acrylic on canvas, 72 × 96 × 3 ¾"

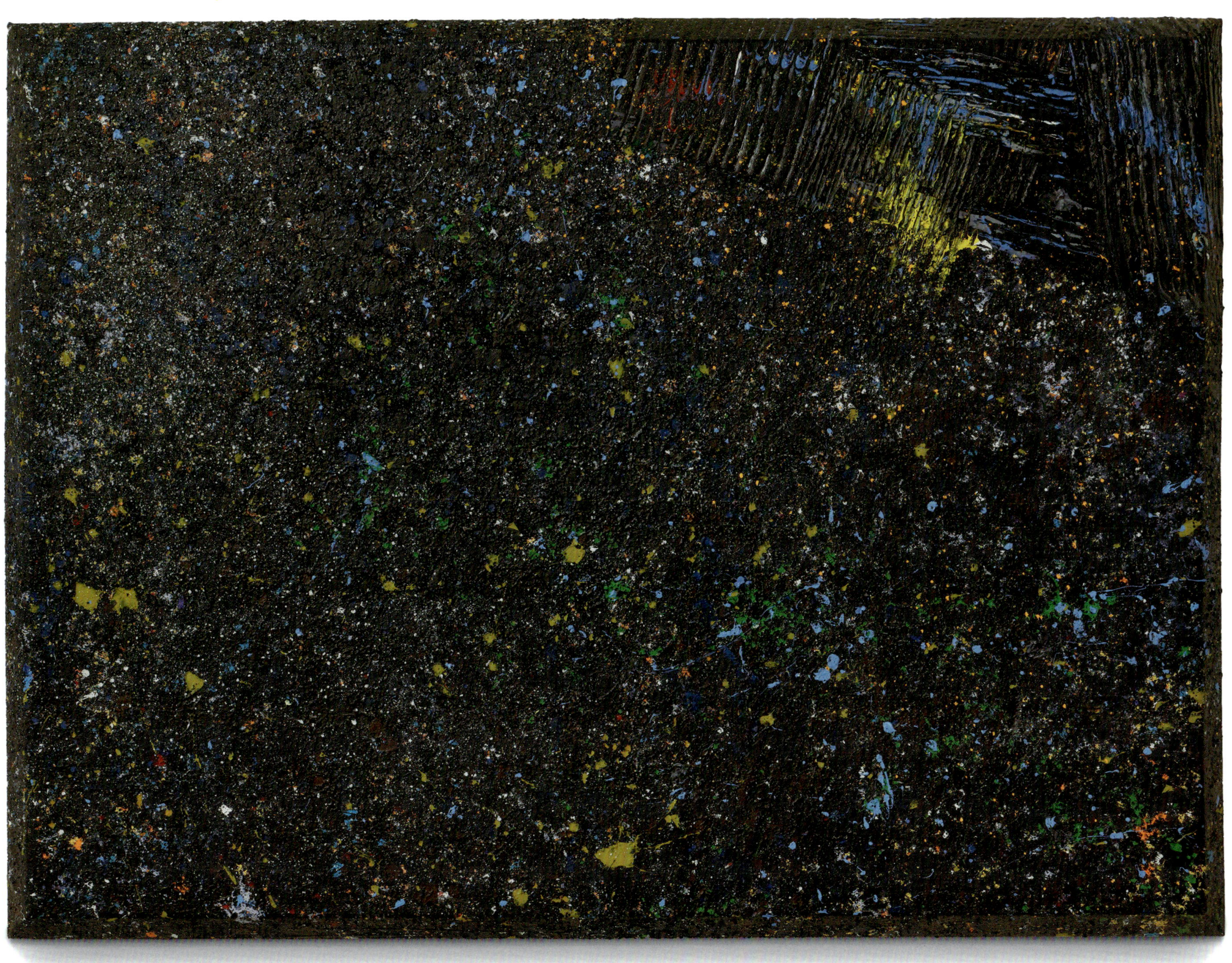

Any Minute Now | 2020 | acrylic on canvas, 96 × 96 × 3 ¾"

A New Generation | 2020 | acrylic on canvas, 72 × 96 × 3 ¾"

October 18 | 2020 | acrylic on canvas, 8' × 20' × 3 ¾"

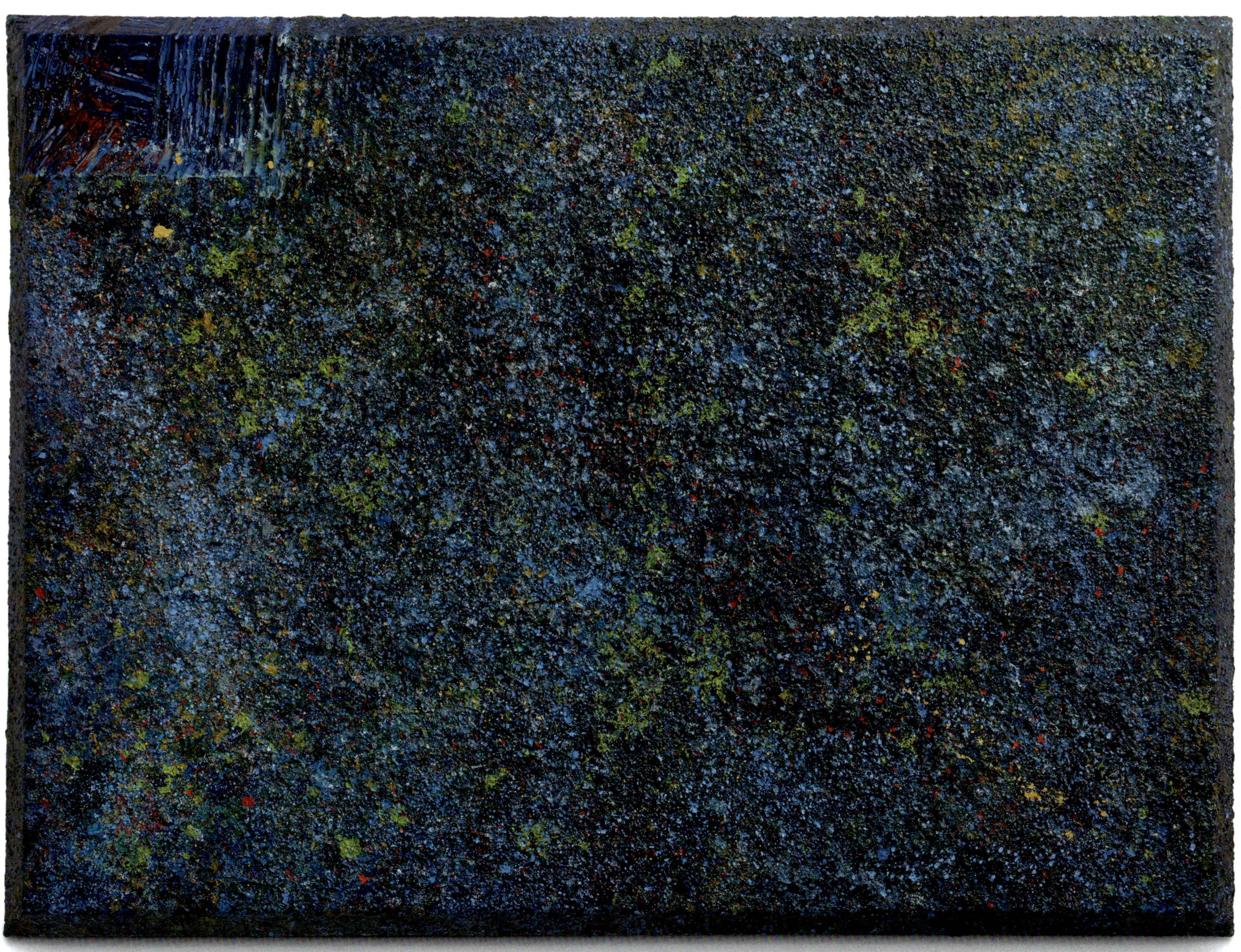

Waiting for "Dutchman" | 2020 | acrylic on canvas, 96 × 96 × 3 ¾"

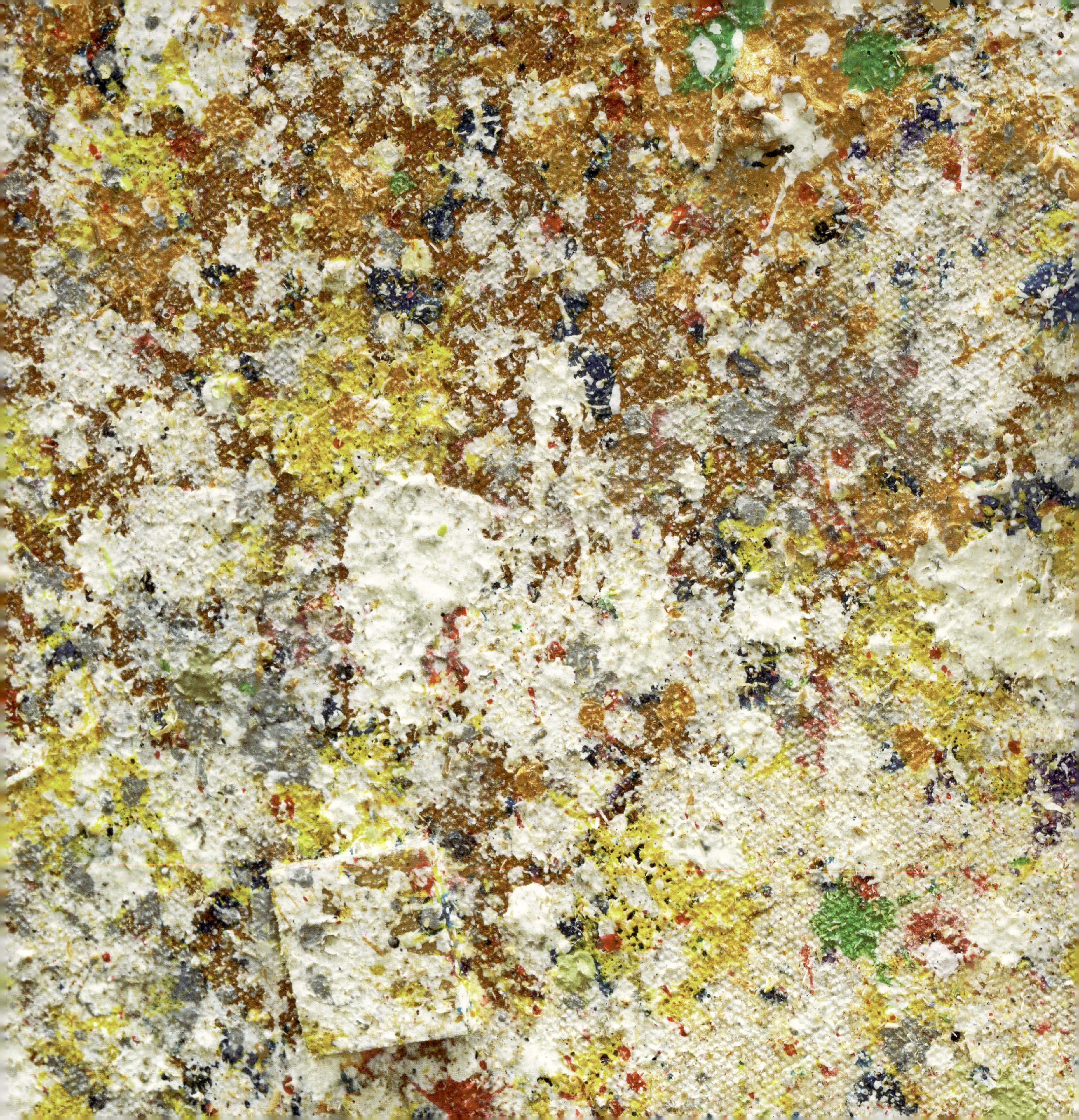

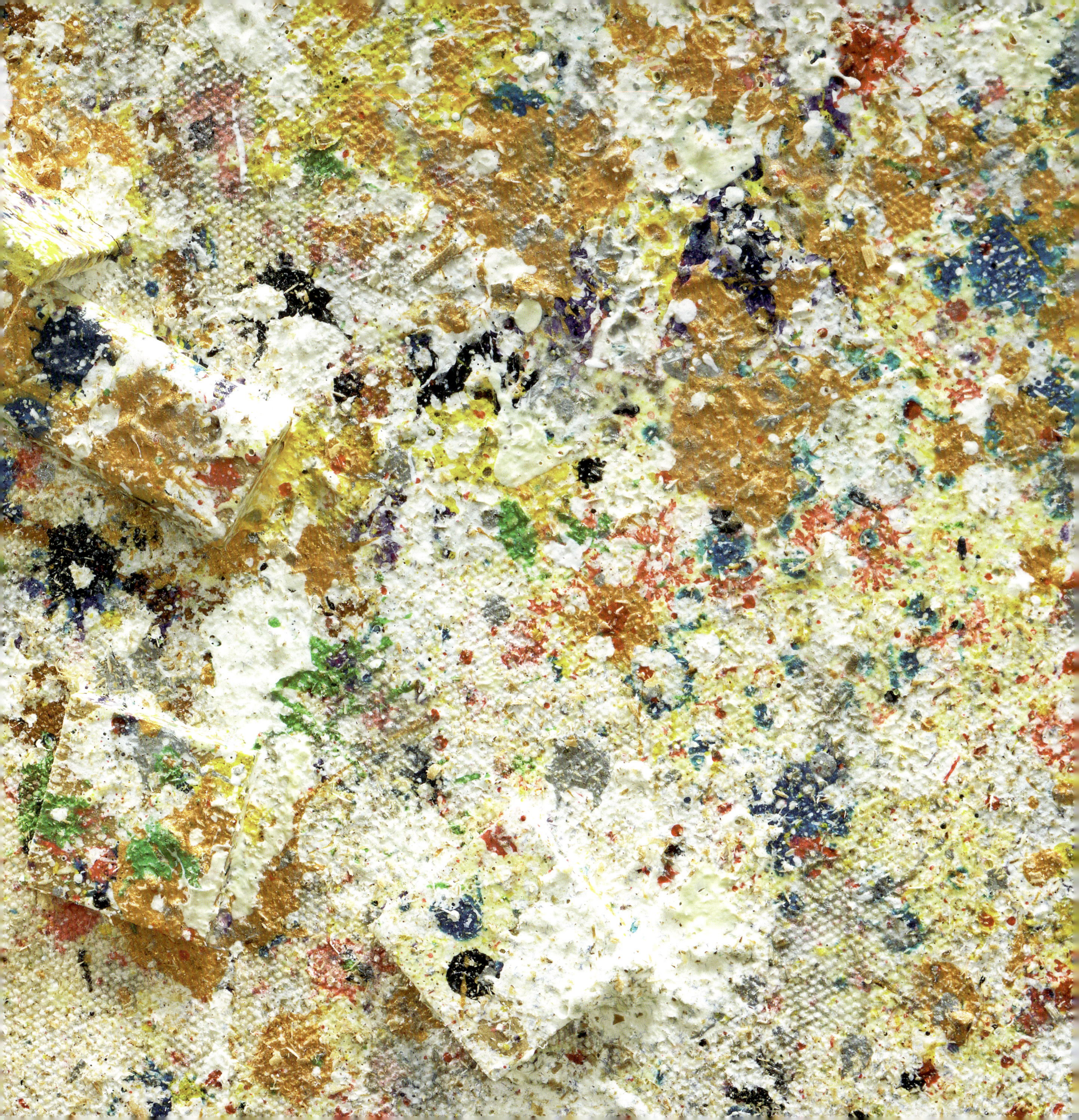

The Mississippi "Shake Rag" | 2020 | acrylic on canvas, 96 × 96 × 4 ¾"

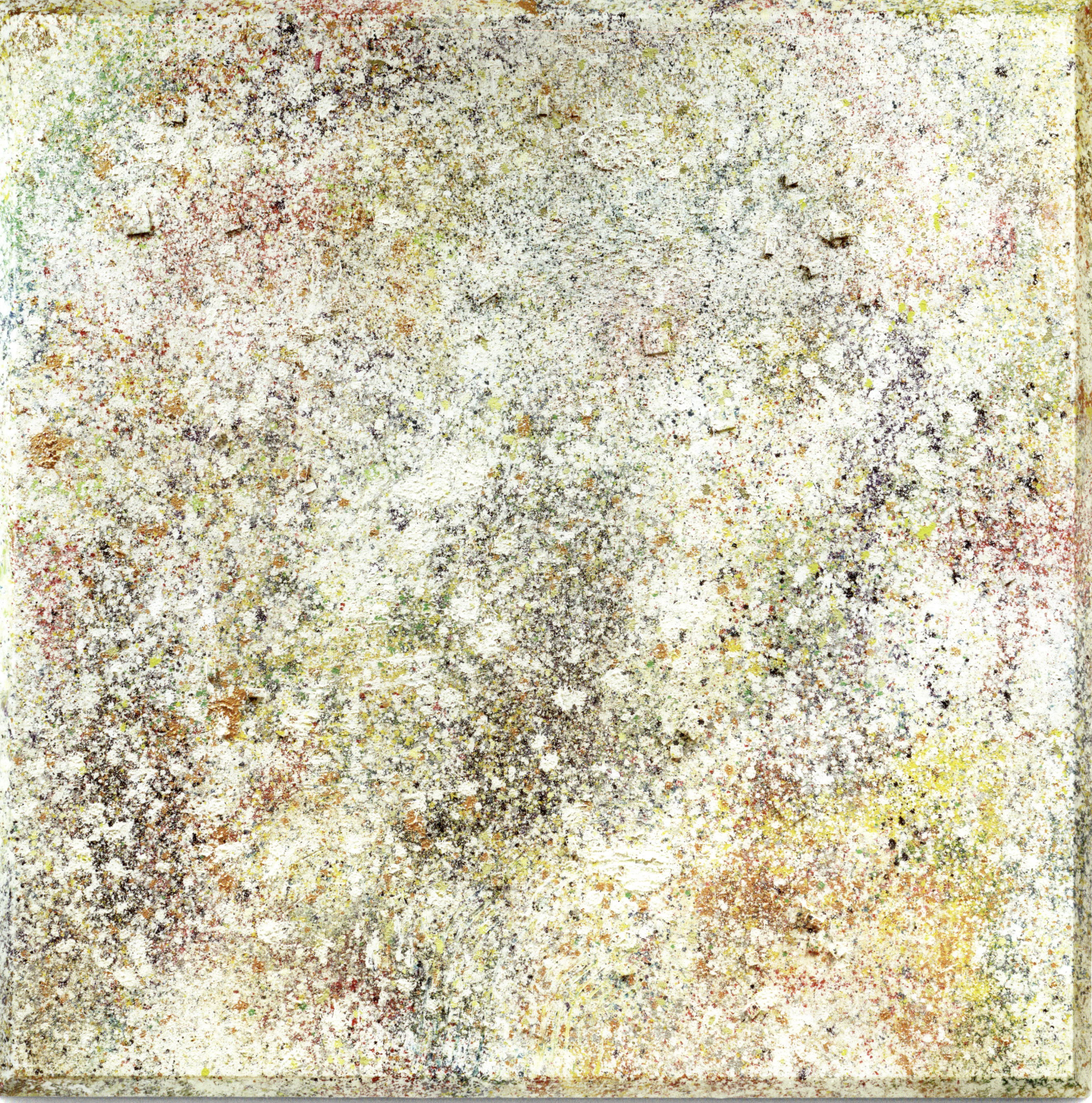

Purple Orpheus | 2020 | acrylic on canvas, 72 × 96 × 3 ¾"

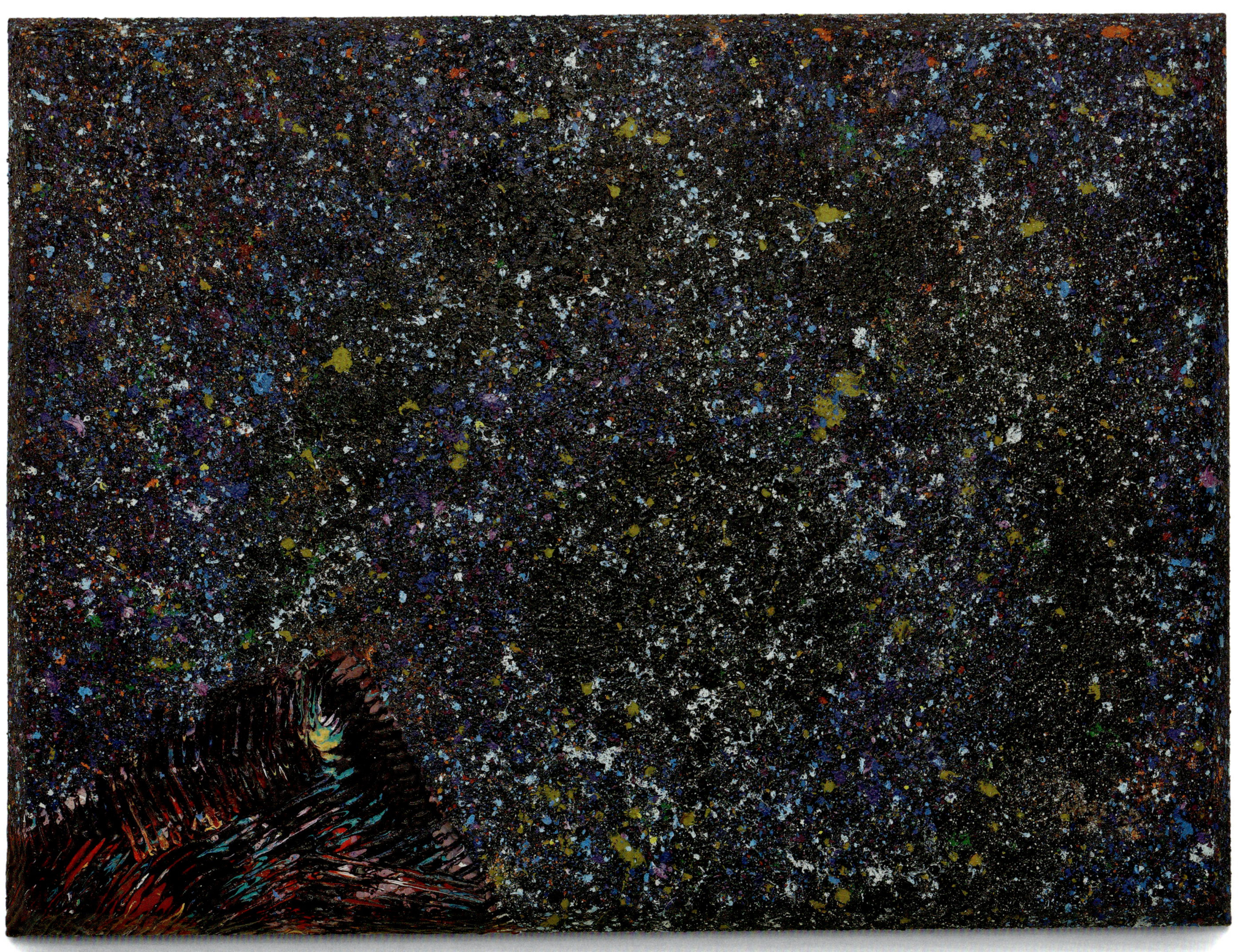

Nikki Giovanni | 2020 | acrylic on canvas, 96 × 96 × 3 ¾"

They Dance and Sail Away | 2020 | acrylic on canvas, 8' × 20' × 3 ¾"

It is Through
US
The Artist
change
Growth
making it wonderful
Sam Gilliam

Hans Ulrich Obrist

A Conversation with Sam Gilliam

December 1, 2019, Washington, DC & June 16, 2020, Skype

Family Life and Finding Art through Music

Hans Ulrich Obrist I read that your father was a carpenter. Can you tell me more about your upbringing?

Sam Gilliam My dad was a good carpenter. Yeah. He wasn't a real carpenter, but he was very aggressive in doing things, like building houses and churches. He did everything: he was a farmer, a baseball pitcher, a deacon, a janitor. He was born in Mississippi, in the Delta, which is a very rich source of music—Mississippi John Hurt, Muddy Waters, all those great singers and guitarists. They made work songs.

The memory of my father became more meaningful when I became much older. I tend to think that he was a great guy. He was beautiful. Wonderful. Very strong. He said I asked too many questions. He is who I became. I always thought that being one of the youngest in the family that I saw more, I saw it from a different position. Now that I'm older, I've passed those kinds of responsibilities on to my kids. One day he said, I'm so proud of you. That was so important. I feel the same about my kids, my relationship, my friends—I'm proud of them.

HUO How did you come to art? How did art come to you?

SG Good teachers, that was probably the most wonderful thing of all. I was number seven in a family of eight: five girls, three boys. That whole picture of what it's like to be a family always plays out: it's that old, generational theory that says if you have a lot of kids, you always have someone to do the work.

My first inclination was to run away from home. Most members of my family were musical—my sisters had singing groups, and we all sang in church. Baptists go to church at nine o'clock in the morning for Sunday School and then eleven o'clock service. Then you have to go back for Baptist training union, the doctrine, and then midnight service. Your Sunday is fully tied up in religious worship. Obviously that was something I did not want to do, so this was a family conflict until, finally, I made my move...

> **HUO** Into art, and music played a big role. I'm interested in art–music collaborations. Dan Graham always says: "We can only understand artists if we understand what music they are listening to." Can you talk a little bit about that?

SG I'm interested in art and music and dance. I danced very well—I used to. And I used to play lots of sports growing up: I was a very good high-school football player and baseball player, like my father. I'm more of a music lover than anything else though, probably because it's much more stable. Music was that presence that established a reservoir of thought in me that allowed me to build, to enjoy, to be free.

With a friend who played harmonica, we would perform at parties—better parties because it was a freer time.

The one thing about going to college was that all these memories were constructed. My professor of American Culture asked me what I was going to write about for my term paper, and I said it would be about dance. He replied, "You've got to write about Faulkner's epic of Yoknapatawpha County—the beginning of the history of Mississippi." One of the beauties of that story is that Faulkner set it in my hometown. Not that I knew it at the time. Tupelo, which is also the place of Elvis Presley, is in the northern part of Mississippi, closer to the Tennessee border.

With sons who are musical, the most difficult thing to do on a Saturday night was to keep us in. We had a father who said, "No smoking, no drinking"—I mean all the rules you're given, and the more he had, the more we broke. The most beautiful thing is that whatever the older brother wanted to do, there was nothing like the protection of a younger brother. You got the younger brother with you, so you have an alibi. Dad didn't like dancing in the house or music. But there was a very good phonograph and lots of records.

We knew about Billie Holiday, and all the singers. Kids in the Baptist church were always getting gifts from various members of the church. We'd call them "play mothers," but they were actually people who guided or influenced our thinking. One of my mother's friends, who gave me books, told me that I'd understand Billie Holiday's song "Strange Fruit" one day; it's about lynching. These became subjects of paintings later on—*Lady Day* [1971] and things like that.

The biggest experience for me was a visiting artist coming from Paris, who said that if it wasn't for the music of America, the Nazi concentration camp would have been miserable. In particular they referred to the singer Marian Anderson. And after painting class we'd go to the musical joints in Kentucky where there were visiting bands or a house band playing.

The age restriction for the places we were going to was twenty-one, but we were in there at seventeen. The opening hours of the bars that had music were based upon their ability to serve liquor, which expired at twelve o'clock in some places. But if they served beer, they could stay open until three or six o'clock in the morning. And there were always places afterward where people would gather. If you went out on a Friday night, you didn't come back until Monday morning—there are songs about that, too.

Professors, Peers, and Influences

> **HUO** The other day I came across a very exciting painting by Tom Downing. He's an important painter.

SG He's a great artist. We collect Downing, and any time an artist visits, we talk about how great Downing was. He was the greatest generational influence for younger groups. He was a teacher, but he liked to hang out, which meant that we all went to certain bars downtown. Tom was very argumentative, but argument—which is nothing more than discourse—led us to think about Gainsborough and Titian and Giorgione, who was one of his favorites. And then Kenneth Noland, who had taught at the Catholic University in DC, moved to New York, and they formed the Washington Color School.

HUO I read in an interview you gave that Tom prompted you to do your striped paintings [fig. 1], which brought you to abstraction. What was that epiphany?

SG Like a musician, if you hear music, you practice it. He didn't influence me, he was someone that I had to beat, to compete with, which meant we hung out together. We had one thing in common: our wives. When I would go to Tom's studio, my wife would talk to his wife, Polly, who was a beautiful woman, a writer. She explained to my wife that artists are great, but they're going to starve you: "He's going to go off and paint, paint, paint, and there will be no concern for family or for you. Plus, he's not going to make any money." The sad experience after leaving Tom's that day, from the first step into the street, was my wife saying, "Stop. Don't starve us."

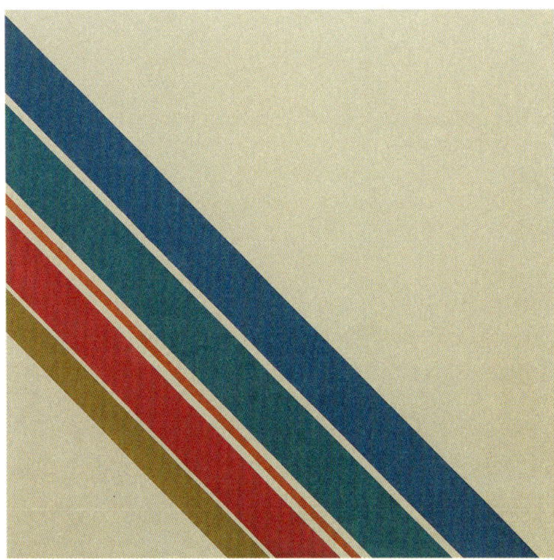

fig. 1
Sam Gilliam
Helles, 1965
acrylic on canvas
71 3/4 × 71 5/16 × 1 1/2"

Tom introduced me to Josef Albers's [practice], which inspired me to teach so I could have time to paint. I taught high school, which was the best thing I could do—I had freedom and was around young people. I was teaching a major art program, which was the first in this part of Northwest, in Washington, DC. I was interested in Barnett Newman and Matisse. Tom's environment was Noland, Frankenthaler, Motherwell.

HUO Can you tell me more about Matisse?

SG I had been taught about Matisse in college, and French painting. One of the fortunate things I had a chance to do was shoot slides for the whole art history department. I saw and ingested all the things that, later, I had a chance to think about. When I was in graduate school the most important visiting professor was Charles Crodel from the Bavarian Academy of Fine Arts.

My professor Ulfert Wilke, an abstract painter, was also important. He spent a lot of time in Japan and was influenced by Mark Tobey, David Parks, and George Weeks. And there was a Spanish painter who taught at Stanford whose paintings, called Walking Men—California figurative paintings derived from Abstract Expressionism—impressed me. Wilke was interested in African art, Colombian art, and Japanese prints. I also spent time in Japan, and the most exciting thing there was the ritual, climbing mountains, Japanese songs, things like this. Within the cultural element of Buddhism, the stillness, etc., you begin to understand the meaning of time as it is stable, as it is constant, as it is moving various aspects. And from that I started making a lot of watercolors.

HUO When did you start the watercolors?

SG I did that in college. If you paint on paper, particularly on a hard surface paper, it pushes back. It holds the color up. The water moves, or it moves with the paper so you can't stop it. You go with the flow, and you don't have to play just for the accidental aspect. You can learn to do deliberate things; you establish your references on the page.

HUO Rainer Maria Rilke wrote this little book, *Letters to a Young Poet*. I was wondering, what would be your advice to a young artist now?

SG You should digest Barnett Newman. Digest the mystery of every artist in the past. Sit and listen to a lecture by a good art historian who puts things in focus. Read books backward. Read books any way you want to. The greatest thing is the play that you had when you were a kid. Maintain that. Of course, right now, the impeachment, the drama, are things that have happened throughout history, but the ability to judge and criticize this time and have your consensus as to how you *want* to be is very important. The whole idea is to exercise your dreams—those things that are in your head, your desires.

HUO Gerhard Richter says that art is the highest form of hope. Do you have a definition of what art is for you?

SG It's possibility. I'd like to form something that is still concrete, and that will change your mind. I don't like Richter. I prefer Anselm Kiefer. Kiefer's work is the most beautiful. He poses the question, "Where's Heaven?" Richter moved too much without real solution. When he came to New York, he came with hopes of making Pop art, but he was confronted by the great Warhol, and Warhol was better, in my mind. But we've learned so much from these artists, and that has changed the dialogue around art.

HUO You were friends with Jack Whitten, Melvin Edwards, and William T. Williams. How was it being associated with that group?

SG It's not what you call Black art; it's actually the openness of art, and this openness was acquired by each of us. I'm the oldest, and Mel and I were the ones that worked off each other. Mel was always the one that referred to Jack. He's shown the most with Mel. And William has shown most with me.

HUO Did you ever have a manifesto or a collective group?

SG No, because I'm singular. The teacher who came from the Bavarian Academy to teach in graduate school would write a lot, and his activity with us was really so important. It has led to the kind of reading that I do now.

HUO I am writing a text on Thaddeus Mosley right now, and he said you've known each other for a long time. Can you talk about your friendship?

SG Thad is the most beautiful artist you'll want to see. He used to be a postman and then a jazz musician and critic. He is actually the soul of Pittsburgh. He's a craftsman woodcarver [fig. 2]. I knew Thad before I came to Pittsburgh—he invited me to the city. He just knew everybody. When I taught at Carnegie Mellon, Thad and I spent more time together. I taught there for five years, mainly because they were being penalized for not allowing Black people to be a part of the university, so they had to hire a teacher who would also be paid a commensurate salary. If I ever got locked out, which I did sometimes at university, I'd go spend the night with Thad. I wrote an essay that got him into his first gallery. That was the beautiful thing about Pittsburgh when the steel mills died: there was the Mattress Factory, there was a celebration of Warhol, there was the Carnegie and the Carnegie International, and then there was Thad. We talk all the time. Thad is the future. We talk all the time.

HUO He also talked a lot about African art and Oceanic art. There is, of course, also a connection of African art with your quilted paintings in the '80s. I wonder if you can talk a little bit about this?

SG Yeah. All of the striped paintings I did after working with Lewis, Noland, and Downing, I gave African titles—cities and things like that. But this was because of Mel, principally, and his first wife, Jayne. They went to Africa together and befriended the poets of Négritude.

HUO Who else has been impactful in your life?

SG Well, I spent a lot of time in Paris with Darthea Speyer—she was the most influential person in my life. She was just the most wonderful, because anything you wanted or had to do, she did for you or you did with her. She made you behave, but she was such a wonderful person. And when I went to Paris, I wanted nothing but to meet Beauford Delaney.

HUO Why was Beauford the artist you wanted so badly to meet?

SG Beauford is the most transitory artist of all. I mean, there's a rumor that he was sent to Paris because he always talked about Monet in New York. The Black artists wanted to talk about Harlem music and things like that, and he was talking about Monet. So they bought him a ticket to Paris. But, I mean, Monet is Monet—Monet is the artist that is the artist. If you could think about Monet and you lived in Harlem, you were alright.

The beautiful thing about Beauford is that he couldn't spend the winters in Paris. His body wouldn't work. So Darthea had to send him to Hydra, Greece. But Beauford is Beauford. His brother paints figuratively, but Beauford does these marvelous abstract paintings and these things that are Beauford. But they are just so beautiful, and the fact is that he was with James Baldwin. They were like a shrine together.

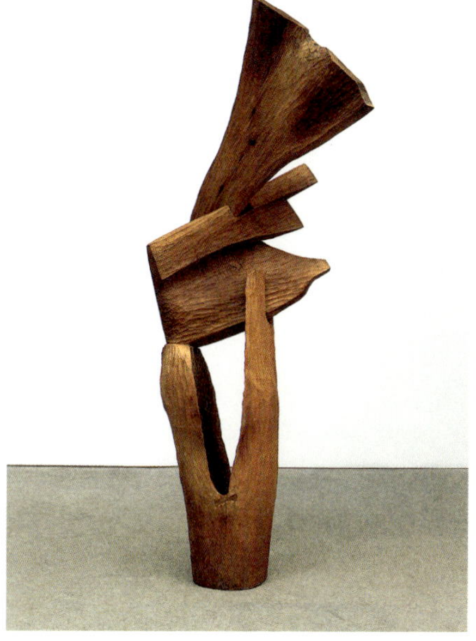

fig. 2
Thaddeus Mosley
Opposing Parallels - Blues Up and Down for G. Ammons and S. Stitt, 2015
walnut
88 × 36 × 28"
© Thaddeus Mosley, courtesy of the artist and Karma, New York

HUO Was Virginia Jaramillo part of your group?

SG Yeah, Virginia Jaramillo, Betye Saar, Barbara Chase-Riboud, Joyce Kozloff, Lynda Benglis.

Virginia Jaramillo and I were in *The De Luxe Show* in 1971 in the Fifth Ward of Houston, sponsored by the de Menil family, curated by Peter Bradley, and directed by Greenberg.

Nancy Graves, who for a time was married to Serra, made paintings, sculpture, prints. We were in some shows together.

Joyce Kozloff is an activist for women's art and in 1970 became involved in the feminist art movement in Los Angeles and New York. She has always represented women artists and worked to promote young artists of that time that should have been elevated.

HUO Are there other artists that you admire?

SG My favorite artist is, of course, Barnett Newman [fig. 3]. There's a list of forty Newman scholars, that's what we are, and one was John Baldessari. Baldessari was one of the most exciting artists. He dealt with script and theater. Many of those artists that came out of Irvine, Baldessari particularly, and Chris Burden, were exciting for artists like Robert Irwin that taught there. It's a perfect example of a different kind of classroom, this sense that there's choreography between the artist and the teacher, you learn from each other.

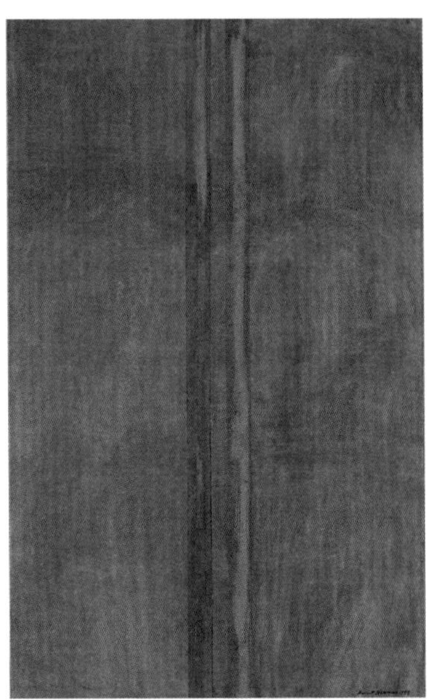

fig. 3
Barnett Newman
Concord, 1949
oil and masking tape on canvas
89 3/4 × 53 5/8"
The Metropolitan Museum of Art, New York. George A. Hearn Fund, 1968
© 2021 The Barnett Newman Foundation / Artists Rights Society (ARS), New York

Slices and Stripes

HUO I went to see your Kunstmuseum Basel show in Switzerland; it was very beautiful. I was wondering about the epiphany you had for these paintings you began in 1967. Before you did them, you did these slices—the beveled-edge-like paintings. What prompted that invention?

SG Shock. If you come to Washington you get a shock. You can understand where Morris Louis came from if you looked at a newspaper with a politician and the American flag on it. You saw what happened to the flag when it was draped. It's a symbol, much like Jasper Johns's target, and Johns's *Flag* [1954–55], following his first target. If you find something that confronts you in art, it can be a generative start. It's that one thing that gets you to begin. And if you establish that initial thing, you can build from it. It's your argument against whatever the conversation about art is at the time—you have to establish yourself with that.

Matisse had that in his Jazz series, or his last series, or the way he moves a leaf within the space, or the transformation he made through color. This presence is called shock. Tom did this by making dots, Noland by making the target, and Louis by making the unfurled paintings, which were very wide paintings with pours at the side. They repeated the ethos of Pollock, which is, "When I paint, I'm in the painting." When the viewer observes the art, he's in the art. He's in the room in which the artist says he's in with the art.

> **HUO** So before you started the Slices series in 1967, where you put acrylic paint on unstretched, unprimed canvas, you were making the stripes.

SG If you're making stripes, you lay out the canvas using masking tape. And if you tape variously you get hard and soft areas, making different markings. The tape will move beyond and you get a stripe of the color. If you loosen the tape, it will move under and cause a mark of how you did things.

That was something that Tom encouraged or praised in my work. If you like an artist, which means you're influenced by them, don't paint what they paint. As long as you learn something from your experience, this is what is positive.

> **HUO** Which is what you did because you then went in a completely different direction with these Slices [fig. 4], where you actually created folds and crumplings.

SG I had to decide to be either what was called a Hard-edge painter or one of those Pollock-like painters, where you just got in there. I really learned from Pollock. I learned to rethink. It meant that in the studio, as opposed to actually painting a canvas that would fit a stretcher, I would just paint on the floor. You paint by choosing the moment, and you can only paint for so long, and within that time that's what you do. It's a part of an attitude of arriving at an end.

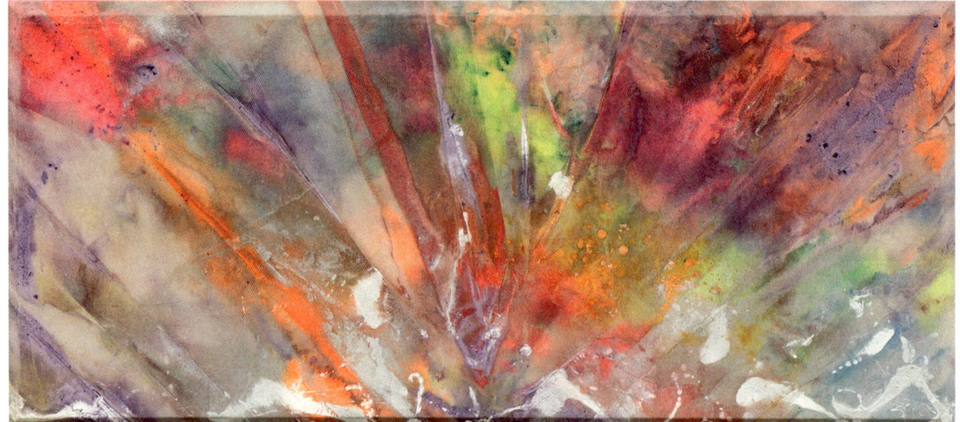

fig. 4
Sam Gilliam
Ray II, 1970
acrylic on canvas
49 × 107 3/8 × 2"

HUO What did you learn from Pollock?

SG Growing up I saw a painting by Pollock that was made on glass so it could be filmed. I saw how he moved around the canvas. How he poured. He created a rhythm. That rhythm is created by movement, and it's done over and over again so that it becomes almost a matrix; it has form. It does something with the space, with the feel. You are then able to see in Pollock your favorite landscape painter, like Bierstadt, which leads you to my painting *Niagara*.

HUO *Niagara* is a great painting because it's very large. I read in an interview with you that one side became so large it fell on the floor. So chance came to the rescue.

SG Once I started painting at thirty to sixty feet—or even three hundred feet—and I started to construct something, I would climb the ladder, and it would fall to the floor. The studio is as much of a performance space as it is a painting space. If you are an Action painter, as Pollock was, or coming out of the Happenings, you performed in the studio—not so much in your physicality, but it was played out in the marks you made.

HUO While you were making the stripes, you also met Walter Hopps. He was a good friend of mine. When I was in my twenties, as a curator at the beginning, I went to meet him in Houston, and I learned a lot from him.

SG Walter came to Washington after escaping the Pasadena Art Museum. He created plateaus, he thought about work, or a situation he was in, and thought about how he could win. He'd position you as a football coach in order to succeed. Walter had such a presence that you never forgot. He helped you establish a sense of purpose. In a way that is how I became an artist: I established intention. I accomplished something that I wanted to do.

First he became director of the Washington Gallery of Modern Art, and then he sold the collection and dispensed it among the artists in the community. His main interest was to create media workshops at Watts Towers in Los Angeles, like in photography, painting, sculpture, and the great one he created was in architecture with a group of architects who immediately left architecture school and built Cadillac Ranch in Amarillo, Texas. He had the ability to involve you in a situation and then give you a focus. Walter also taught you to ramble, and liked to talk about John Coltrane—he mentioned that he liked me because he thought I liked Coltrane, but I really liked Miles Davis better.

HUO Did you meet Coltrane?

SG Yeah, I did. I went to concerts; I saw him play. But really I collected records and would have listening sessions. If someone comes and plays Coltrane, you play Miles Davis, and you play all night long. Or you go to concerts in New York.

HUO You have said that you were inspired by Coltrane because he worked the whole sheet at once, and that's why you work the whole canvas. Can you explain that analogy?

SG Any painting has a shape. If you played Coltrane's "My Favorite Things," it was done in time. On the record, it always tells you the time that the composition lasts—it's about five minutes. And it's like standing watching a train: you wait for the cars to go by, and depending on whether it's passenger or commercial, you see from a stable point—you see this movement and music. Coltrane did that same thing: he would play, and you could hear him breathing. No one would give me credit for being a musicologist or understanding music, but it taught me how to paint. It's time that matters: listening and realizing what happened with the music, my experience of sound established these references in painting.

One of the things with the show I did with Walter in 1969 is that he challenged me to work in spaces thirty by sixty feet—an old Victorian space with high ceilings. He said, "You're going to have to build a hell of a lot of stretchers to work that size." I said, "Not me."

We ordered a hundred yards of canvas, and I worked on the third floor—I had a lift. I could put the canvas in twenty-five-yard sections, which I'd then paint. I would do it like those processes of origami, or even ritual games I would play as a kid, like cat's cradle, a game with strings. All these became a means of folding the canvas before I painted it. It's not so much folding; it's orchestrating the canvas. If you paint a canvas that has been pleated, you take the canvas and you lap it; there's an undulating rhythm. With media surface breakers, which means having a wetting agent that goes through, you can paint completely by controlled accident. You can throw the paint. With acrylics there are chemicals, hardeners, transparent agents, and agents that allow you to paint color on top of color so that you can make the painting within a few hours. The beautiful thing is that the preparation is just as exciting—like a surgeon.

Poetry, Prints, and Collages

HUO You mentioned in the article I read that you don't sleep.

SG I go to sleep, but I wake up, and I'll have the whole night and then go to sleep. I've always done that. I'm hard to wake up in the morning. I was always awake when my brother got up to deliver his papers. My father rang the bell for the church when someone died, so I would go over to him. Sometimes I'd sleepwalk—I would even leave the house, go across the street, and be found sitting on the church steps. But I learned to control that. And these become passive affinities—whatever I do during the day, whatever I'm working on, I dream about at night. I learned to use that.

HUO Do you write down your dreams?

SG I write poetry.

HUO Has your poetry been published?

SG One poem was once used in an exhibit. My wife also keeps records. I have a section at home in the basement, which is my studio, with poetry books. When I'm in the studio alone, I record my thoughts and refer to the poems and poets that I like: E. E. Cummings's "The Acrobat Passage" and *The Enormous Room*, Neruda's *Twenty Love Poems*, Dylan Thomas, or John Ashbery. All those poets of free iambic pentameter, or no iambic pentameter.

HUO It's amazing that you write so much poetry. I would love to read it.

SG In high school, there were no art programs, so you became an English major. These sorts of things warm you up: they release the painting activity. The letters that I write or the poems I've done for people, I like to use them as drawing.

HUO You also make gigantic prints, like the ones you showed in Korea.

SG Eight one-hundred-yard paintings that were run through a press for the Art in Embassies Program. We did eight events with each painting in four different countries. Once I was in each place I would find things that would accent the room, and we'd build with these elements. That's the way I learned to approach paint: painting is an interior; it's a volume, a vessel in some way.

HUO An interior vessel.

SG Yeah, and you react to what you find in that placement of the target on the wall. When I first bought the studio there was a sawhorse. So, I tried to build something intentionally, and I put buckets of paint on the sawhorse, and then I had this thing like a mountain. Or when I see a mountain, this thing happens in space, a gesture in space, a shock. If I could paint that shock, I'd be a good artist!

HUO To paint that shock, that's really good. Another thing that is exciting is that your spray paintings are never hung in the same way twice. You once said, "It's like music. When you play a music piece, you never play it twice the same." Is that correct?

SG It depends on the auditorium, on the concept. We've come now to this idea of performance. I should be active near the painting, in the space and the sweep of the space, and I have to determine how the person viewing it moves, like the composer Modest Mussorgsky.

Even though we're all influenced by Joseph Beuys, he wouldn't be who he was if it weren't for Caspar David Friedrich or Dürer—through this activity that happens throughout the media of art. The fact is sometimes, though you work in the present, you are going back. You can do it both as part of a past experience or trying to work toward something new. The way that we reference period after period changes; it gets the same sort of treatment that you get in paintings: if you do one show, the next show has to be different.

HUO So each one is a new chapter; it's a new method; it's a new work.

SG It has to be different parts. The studio keeps some diaries, and my wife catalogs, so we can go back through the years and see what we're doing.

HUO Also, sometimes you experiment with collages. What prompted you to make the black paintings and geometric collages?

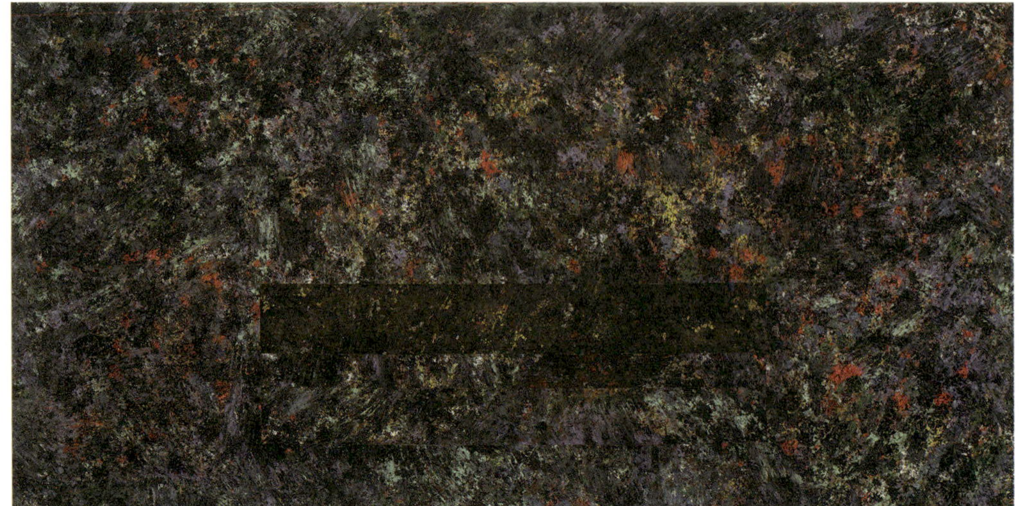

fig. 5
Sam Gilliam
Rail, 1977
acrylic and canvas on canvas
90 ¾ × 180 ¾"
Hirshhorn Museum and Sculpture Garden, Smithsonian Institution, Washington, DC. Museum Purchase, 1978

SG Well, Cubism, Constructivism, Mondrian, the interaction between Mondrian and the colors on a grid, and the painting of Braque. The sense of painting as volumetric—the painting that unifies itself between painting and sculpture, or when you see the wall and the floor. In the black paintings there was always the center—cutting it out and putting it back, but sometimes it's just turning it upside down. If I took that rectangular part out, I had parts that had white substances to it.

But the real thing about the black paintings is that I finally made a piece that only started in black and actually opened up to this. I developed it around the collage by taking out the point of center, so the painting took the idea of collage and made it into a visual whole in a much freer way.

It's interesting that it's called *Rail* [fig. 5]. It's a large painting. If you paint, make a painting, or make a show, the show is transitional. It's not the same.

HUO It has a limited lifespan.

SG Right. You try to build the method by which to tell the story, the drama of how you want the show to exist in terms of the space.

New Work

HUO What is the process with your new painting?

SG It's not finished yet: it has to be picked up, thrown into position, then painted, and then brought back to a final color. It's going to be a red painting. We start with white, just by pouring paint, and it's glazed over. Then we'll pull the painting into a physical shape and paint that. That will give it a start and stop. It marks an empty feeling. And then we will try to paint that structure into something that is singular and stretch it.

HUO So it becomes holistic in the end?

SG Yes, it becomes both whole and theatrical.

HUO You have also made a new series of works on paper, so I wanted to ask you to tell me a little bit about them.

SG They are seventy-nine inches square, thereabouts. And there's some color and an image that you have to find by looking at it, you discover it. It's not obvious.

HUO So it's an image the viewer has to find.

SG Yeah.

HUO I saw your beautiful exhibition at the Flag Art Foundation. Those works were very much about solid and transparent paint with a lot of blending, and it seems that these are more monochromatic.

SG Yes. The paper absorbs more, so you have to maintain the surface quality. One thing is that with the number of pieces of paper, color alone cannot be the identity, so there has to be some way of distinguishing one from the other. However, whenever I work on it, I don't want to destroy the green, the blue, the red, the yellow.

HUO There was an interview in the *Brooklyn Rail*, and the interviewer visiting your studio, Tom McGlynn, saw some of these newer works and said they are more hard-edged, more monochromatic. Are they more hard-edged?

SG They are. Everything is geometric, and the color is used in a way that is equal. Most of the larger works are made of wood—one is eight feet in diameter—so the color builds the visual relationship. Most paintings are black or white, and, thus, the color in the space establishes a different moment or presence. It's just there.

HUO You also said that they are more structured, like *completely* structured. Can you talk a little bit about this aspect of them?

SG Yeah, there are circles and squares, and by that I mean they have a form, and that form corresponds to other forms. At the moment, I'm trying to be subtle, and it's something that you have to find, that you have to establish yourself. The problem is that nothing is new. So why not make it fun?

HUO They're very different from the previous ones I saw at the Flag Art Foundation. But do you make them in the same way?

SG The ones at Flag were folded, much like free concepts of origami. And the paint is poured through the folds, which sometimes may be from the back. And then there's a surface that is painted directly. Because there are agents that cause the paint to flow, or other things added, an accidental process happens that only occurs when the paint dries, or in the drying process. There's a lot of movement, though it's controlled for the fold, so when you open it up, it's there. The real thing is not to have control of what happens, just to set it into motion. It's not to be exact so they can arrive at something.

HUO In the previous ones, there is a lot of unexpected, almost accidental blending; in these new ones is it more controlled? Is there less accident?

SG Yeah. The new work is hard to make because the aim is not to lose the materiality of the paper that I'm working with. Whatever I do, the surface has to have that texture, so everything seems to reside inside the paper, which is very thin, very large, and, obviously, architectonic—built to exist in the space, built to be realized, not built to be perfect.

HUO You've also made some new watercolors. They are beautiful. They're watercolors on...?

SG On rice paper.

HUO They have amazing colors.

SG All the colors that are mixed are very strong. They're either very strong in color and intensity or they're strong in concentration of pigment. Most of them are vertical, which means that they're then a consideration of how they're going to operate in the space.

HUO You once said that purple is your favorite color. Do you still have a favorite?

SG I'm more didactic: red, yellow, blue, black, and white. I choreograph the color in terms of the way I want it to be seen. I write these colors out in a sequence of what the painting's going to be.

HUO So you're quite systematic.

SG Yeah. Well, actually, it's what I want to be seen in the space. It's all Mussorgsky. I want these visual elements. There are a lot of musicians that I actually react to.

HUO Can you talk a little bit about your new body of work using dyed lumber?

SG I'm looking for union, unity, even though the black has to be transparent because it has to reveal the structure of the wood. Most of the wood is parallel to the floor, and it comes from a block, which starts out in a radical form. All of the pieces have a band, and as you go around them, it changes. Dyeing, as such, allows the wood grain to exist with whatever shape you have, and is established by your examining it. If you get close to the block, it seems to be leaning over you—maybe I'm too impressed by mountains! You won't climb it; you'll see it. You'll fill it.

HUO As far as I understand the pieces are going to be eight feet high, which is very large.

SG That's only one piece. If it's possible to put the cap on the eight feet, we may have to dislocate the other dimension. But you could imagine that they go together, they go together and almost touch the sky, as personified by the room.

HUO When I was in your studio the surfaces were still wet. You were working on it, and it seemed that they were dyed like stains.

SG The staining is to clarify how it's made. How you are supposed to see it and react to it; it's recognizable. You have to move in order to see it, as in dance.

HUO Walter Hopps always told me that Duchamp would talk about the viewer doing the work, or doing half of the work, or maybe even more than half of the work. And it seems that with this dance you describe, the viewer is very involved and doing part of the work.

SG It's true, and in a sense the viewer discovers themself. You are who you are, or you become what you aspire to become. It's the presence of an object within a room, within a space, its relationship with things like this that the viewer defines. And he better do a perfect job. I mean, it's about them. What do they say? What you see is what you get.

HUO In terms of what you see is what you get, when you were describing your piece *Rail*, you said that it's a visual whole. How would you describe this visual whole?

SG You see it mostly by seeing it. It becomes whole in terms of the experience of what you make of it. When it's built in a space, you see it, you think about it.

Future and Unrealized Projects

HUO You've worked with architecture and large-scale public art, and that's, of course, so important. We need a new form of public art now, particularly in the current moment—almost like a new movement. It's inspiring to look at the many public artworks you've been creating—for Philadelphia, you did *Seahorses* [1975, fig. 6] for Art in Architecture, for example—and you once said that the Eiffel Tower is an inspiration. Do you have any other large-scale projects planned?

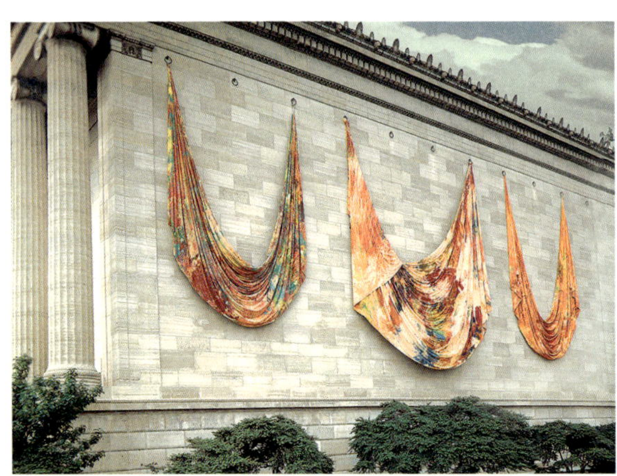

fig. 6
Sam Gilliam
Seahorses, 1975
Installation view at Philadelphia Museum of Art, April 26–May 25, 1975

SG I have a bid in for a project at the new Grand Central Station, which I find interesting because I love trains. It's going to be a mosaic. If this station had been in New York at least two to four thousand years ago, it would have been under water. In reading and writing and talking, we have to have this shock of our consensus.

HUO It goes back to this shock.

SG Yeah, and you want consensus. When the viewer sees it, you want them to be hit by experience and delighted.

HUO It's a portal.

SG Yeah, and when we do these projects outdoors, people can come and watch the whole thing being installed. The idea is to establish contact. I have done a lot of public projects because they are a way of paying for my experiences as a professional artist. Becoming aware of the drama of working with architects, architectural students, and studio assistants on the projects is also an experience. You go there and, much like an architect—it's architectonic—you build it. Winning prizes means you're good, but the real thing is in the organization of the team that you're working with.

HUO I'm also interested in unrealized projects, like your Times Square piece. What did you want to do there?

SG Times Square was going to be at the entrance to the train station. We had a project that was to exist as a track base and would simply place elements of movement along the base.

HUO Do you have any dream projects?

SG I have always wanted to do a park. There's Central Park, and there's a beautiful park on 16th Street that has a waterfall.

HUO What does your garden look like?

SG We've got twelve trees—we planted them in the front and back and they bloomed. Our place is also right up against Rock Creek Park, which is full of trees, the park is an oasis. Late at night, if you wake up, it's just flat black with structures; it's Surrealistic. It's nice to wake up to that and then go back to sleep.

It's a prelude to what the studio is like. Luckily, much of the work is fabricated, which means that I work with a person who can build, so I don't see the work, I see the drawings. But the growth of the work is involved with the things that I focus on as my work happens. Right now it's the presence of these really dark trees against the paint at night. I just sit here and wait and contemplate and understand where I'm going. I carry my art with me. I mean, anything that we see while moving or that happens to us—our politics, maybe—is our consciousness of our presence on earth, and it's about how that affects us, how we react to it.

Art and Politics

HUO César Domela was a friend of mine, and he was friends with Mondrian. He said Mondrian was actually very political. Domela told me just because his work is abstract doesn't mean it's not political. You once said the same thing—you always said that your art is political.

SG It's only a point of view, but it's also the most positive and peaceful point of view. The most beautiful thing is to read the *New York Times* and the *Washington Post*, and your favorite critics have already resolved what's going to happen. The Democrats have these

fig. 7
Sam Gilliam
Green April, 1969
acrylic on canvas
98 × 271 × 3 7/8"
Kunstmuseum Basel, Switzerland

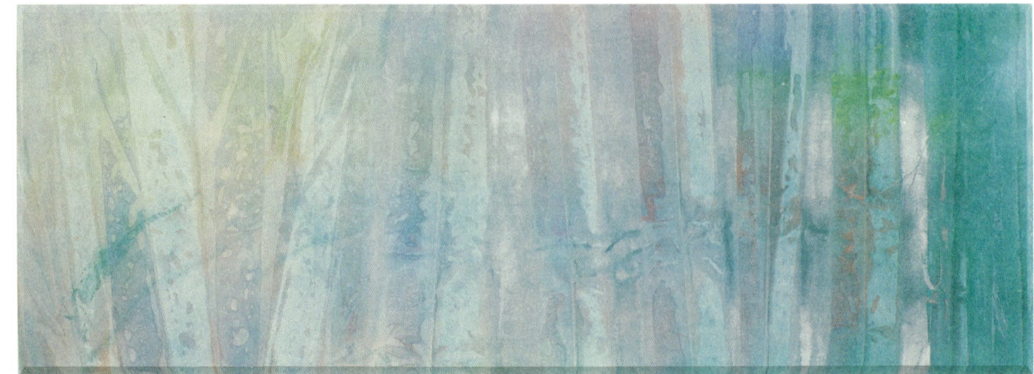

simultaneous debates where the great few are reacting to what they can do in terms of what will actually be our respective future.

HUO In some of the paintings, you have political content—for example, in *Green April* [1969, fig. 7]. Can you tell me about that piece?

SG Well, I used to work with the NAACP, and the March on Washington was in April. And April 4 was the date Martin Luther King died in 1968. It's also a tradition in Jewish philosophy to mourn for a year and then commemorate the date. I've done a *Red April* [1970] and a *Green April*, and just stopped the series.

HUO You mentioned the Watts Towers earlier, and that, of course, brings us back to 1965, where a roadside argument escalated to police violence. Can you talk more about politics in your art?

SG Well, everyone looks for a system, and politics causes us to relate to a particular thing. Why not art? It's harmless. It doesn't bother you. It causes you to think. It causes you to progress. And politics is simply a way of existing. It may be controlling sometimes when it occurs in this era. Art is something that is present because it's in memory. It surpasses time, boundaries, and continuation. It means that this political situation, which can seem imprisoning, is actually not confining.

HUO When you were asked in an interview recently about why abstract art is political, you said it challenges you and the viewer to understand something that is different, and it convinces you that what you think isn't everything. Can you explain that to me?

SG An idea is a challenge. It's your motivation. It doesn't have to be violent. You don't have to hurt, burn, yell, do anything. It's interesting now that with the demonstrations at this time, which are about Black Lives Matter, the coach of the Atlanta Hawks basketball team made a very good statement: you don't have to kill people just because they are sleeping; you don't have to kill people if they run away. There is a better way to act. There's a better way to be. The coach said he develops basketball players to play, to win, to be themselves through practice. They enjoy the game. And no matter how fiercely they play, they have to shake hands again at the end. You work hard. You have a direction. But you don't kill. You don't try to master control. That's good politics.

The Exhibition

HUO What's the title of the show at Pace Gallery?

SG *Existed Existing*. As in, you weren't there, but here it is—for your information, here it is.

HUO Historically your work has been very specific for and connected to each space. Has your latest work been prompted by Pace's new space?

SG It is definitely connected to the space, but it's connected to the space as you see it, as you want to see it, and as you want others to see it. There has to be space, of course, for a person or people, but it's going to be a dance. It's going to have an expression because it's architectonic, which means it's going to be built for that particular space.

HUO Let's talk about this idea of the exhibition being a dance.

SG It's controlling people's movement. There are only certain ways you can move through the dance and build your rhythm, which will be controlled by the way that things are placed on the walls or in the space. The word "dance," in that sense, doesn't mean a particular thing. It's free.

In terms of other works of mine, these pieces are more resolved. Less in terms of color, because the color will only be black and white. With an aluminum piece that sort of changes the aspect of the blackness or the whiteness—there's something subtle, something not there.

HUO In the exhibition, there is also going to be a series of circular wall works. Can you tell me about those?

SG They are a response to this idea of the pyramid. I realized that the exhibition would be better defined by the works on the wall, which refer to large, circular color. This discovery of these exact relationships allows you to enjoy the dance—to think, to move, and hopefully, to buy! It has a certain organization. It really is a pretty good solution to things that I've been about all along. Clarity. It exists.

HUO And then there is one work that almost seems to be a box with six elements.

SG The abacus is like the table of contents. The idea of pyramids turned into blocks, and the blocks are simply a small sample that changes because they are made to rotate. It's interesting to see one plane against the other as it spins. Suddenly this idea of the abacus became a form of content for larger pieces that I wanted to see a certain way. Actually there are some leftover blocks that became more beautiful than the idea I had for them in the beginning.

I discovered that a block is not a block; it has all sorts of positions. I realized that one thing I had to do, personally, was create a presence to make one block. It just stayed there. I mean, it stayed in space because of the square image. It was like a wall—and much like the wall pieces. It is what it is in terms of the four sides—which way it leans, the way it goes away from you. You walk around it. You find it. It's yours, because it's the content you develop. It's existence. It's the individual nature of the person.

HUO The abacus, of course, is also the calculating tool from lots of different ancient cultures. In this exhibition, will there only be one abacus, or is it a series?

SG We started with a limited edition of abacuses, but they've grown. We started accepting the fact that there were blocks of wood, and that idea transferred into many forms. One becomes many—I'm getting religious. One becomes particular, and one is all you need.

HUO There are endless possibilities, and once more, you really expand that horizon, you expand the language through this exhibition. In a previous conversation you told me that in order to stay alive, you have to keep mobile.

SG Keep moving. Keep growing. Be persistent. Not like some politicians that we know. This dance contest you win by endurance. Through insistence. Through existence, perseverance, and having a point of view.

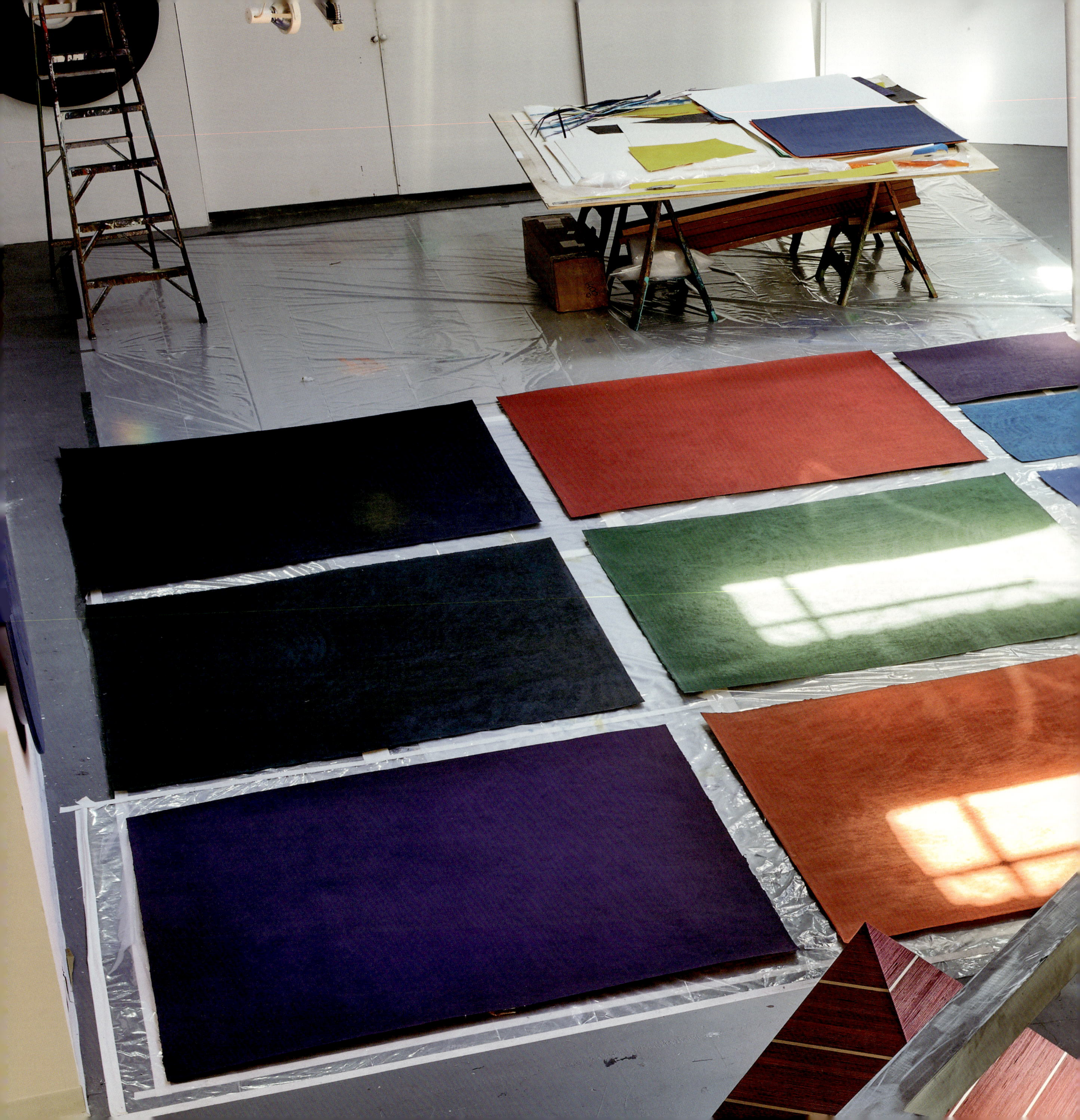

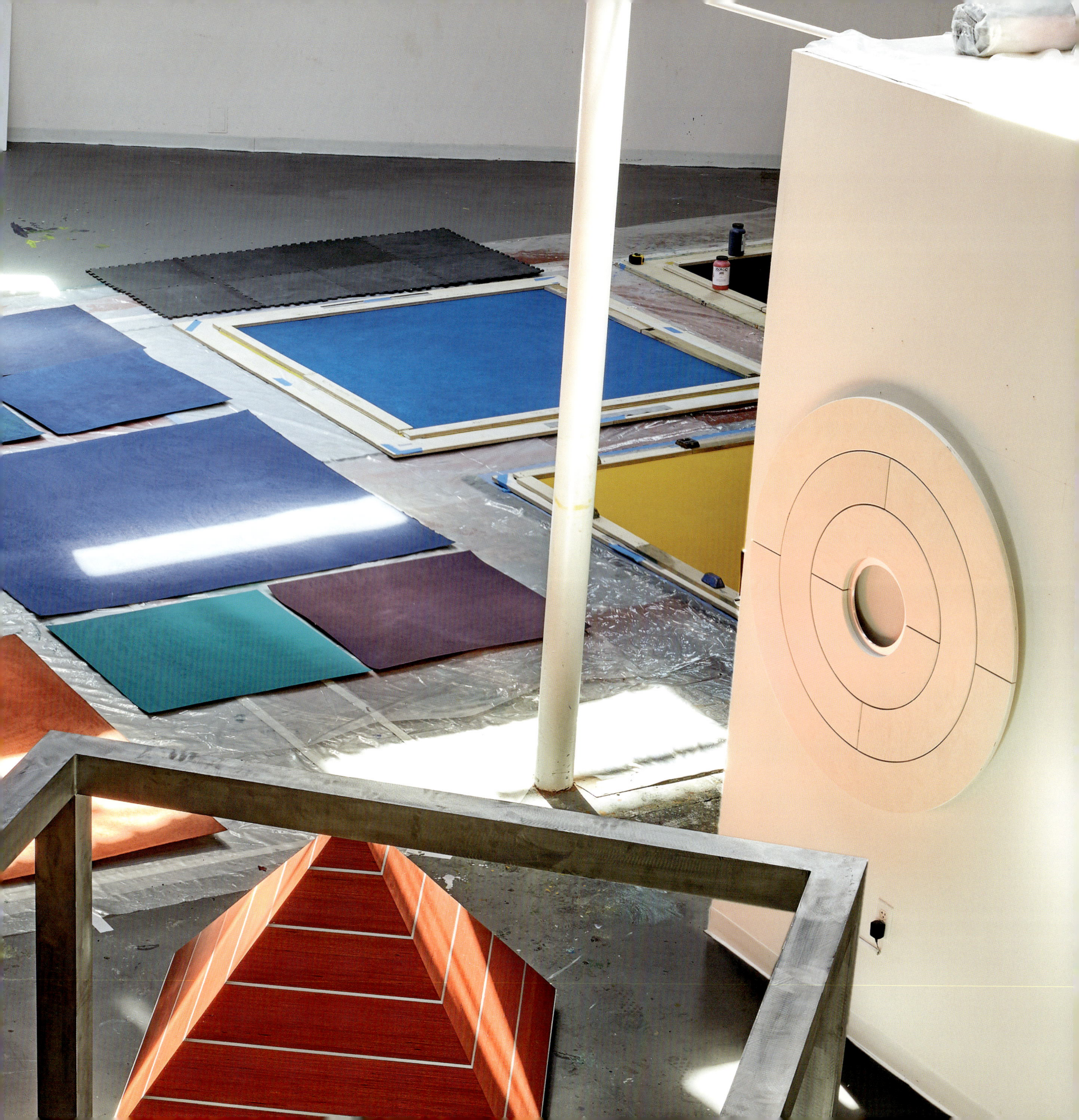

Washi Paper – Yellow | 2020 | acrylic on washi, 79 × 79"

Washi Paper – Purple/Black | 2020 | acrylic on washi, 79 × 79"

Washi Paper – Red | 2020 | acrylic on washi, 79 × 79"

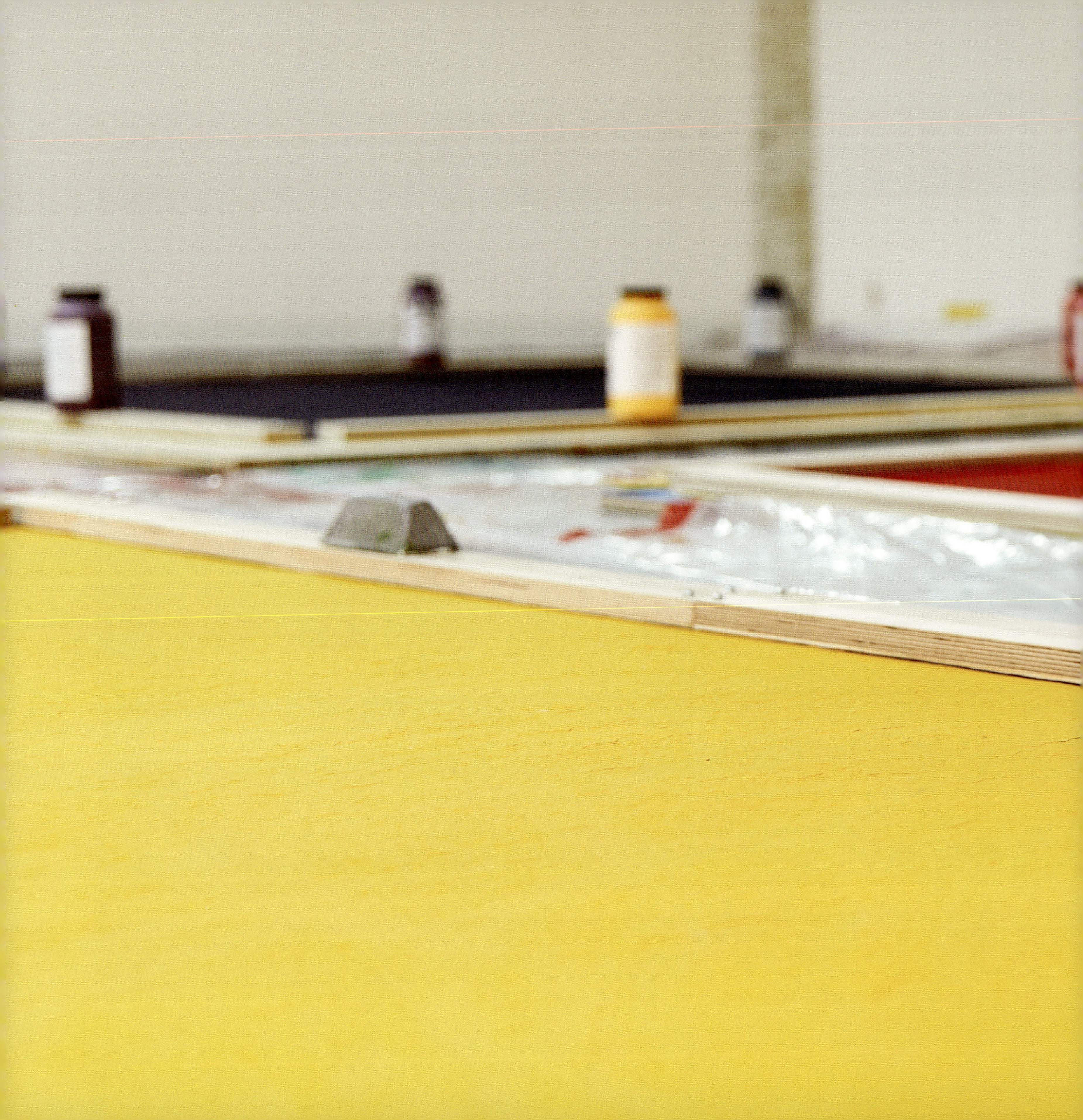

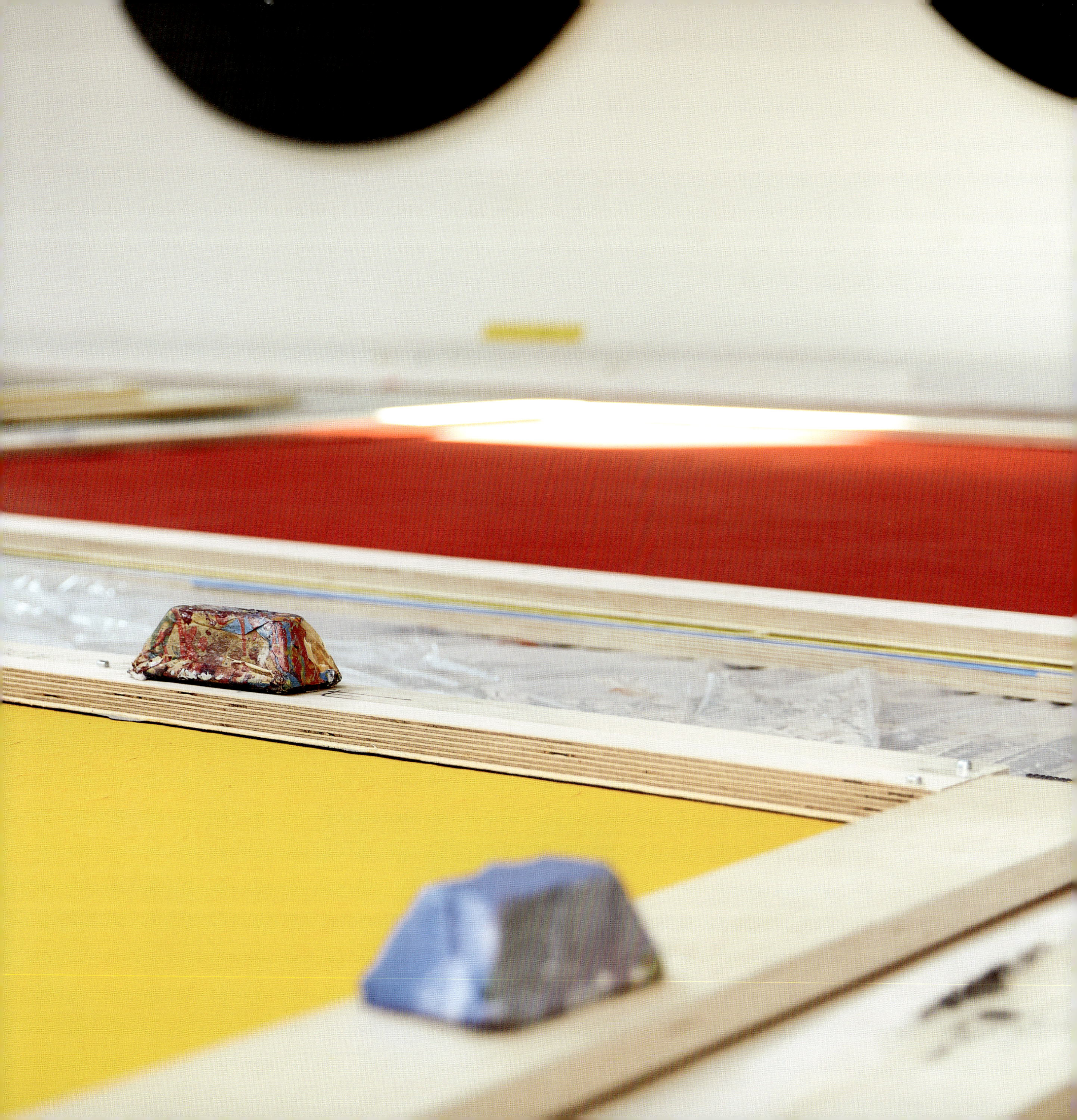

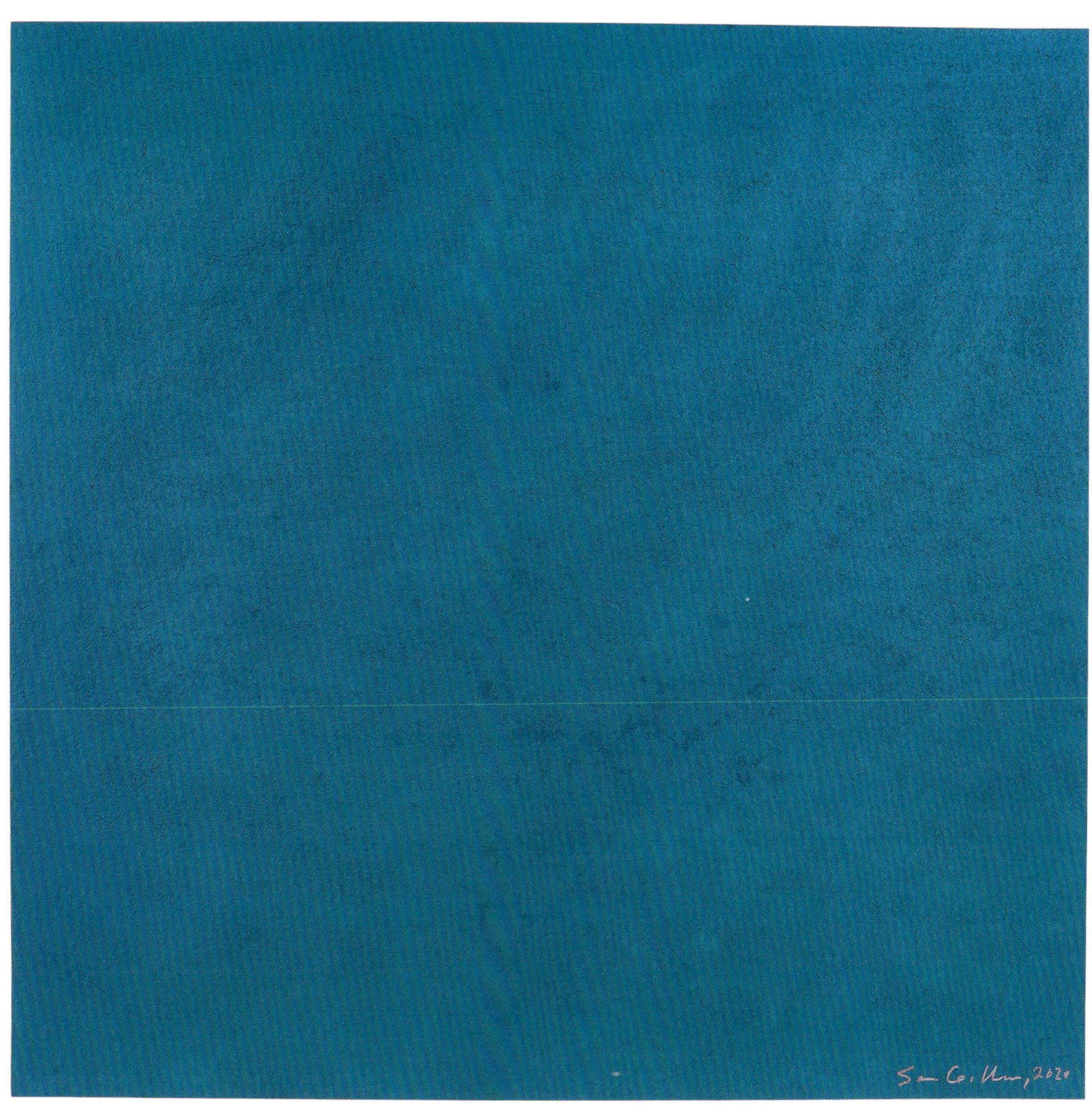

Washi Paper – Turquoise | 2020 | acrylic on washi, 38 ⅝ × 38 ⅝"

Washi Paper – Blue V | 2020 | acrylic on washi, 38 ⅝ × 38 ⅝"

Washi Paper – Orange | 2020 | acrylic on washi, 79 × 79"

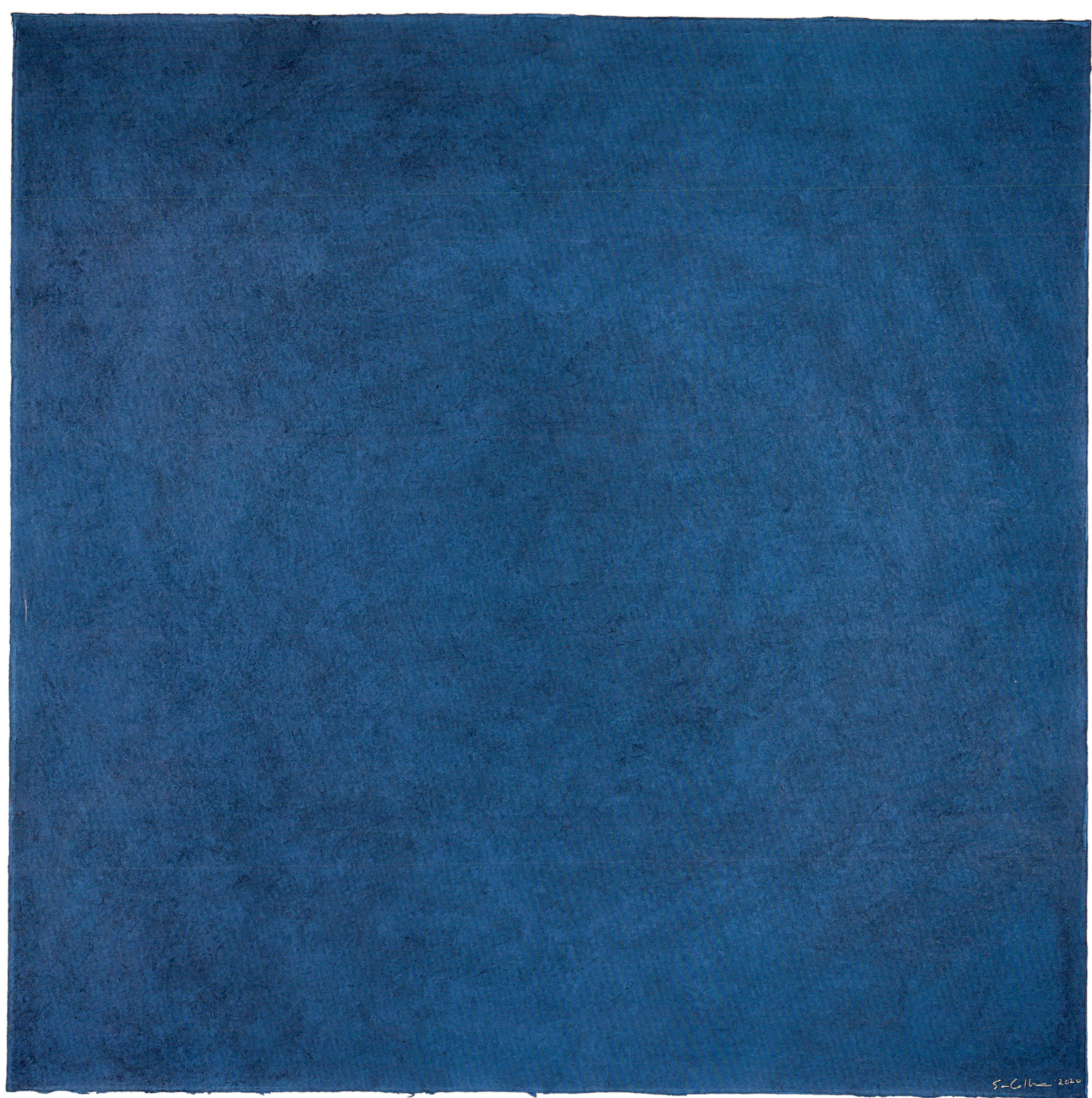

Washi Paper – Purple | 2020 | acrylic on washi, 79 × 79"

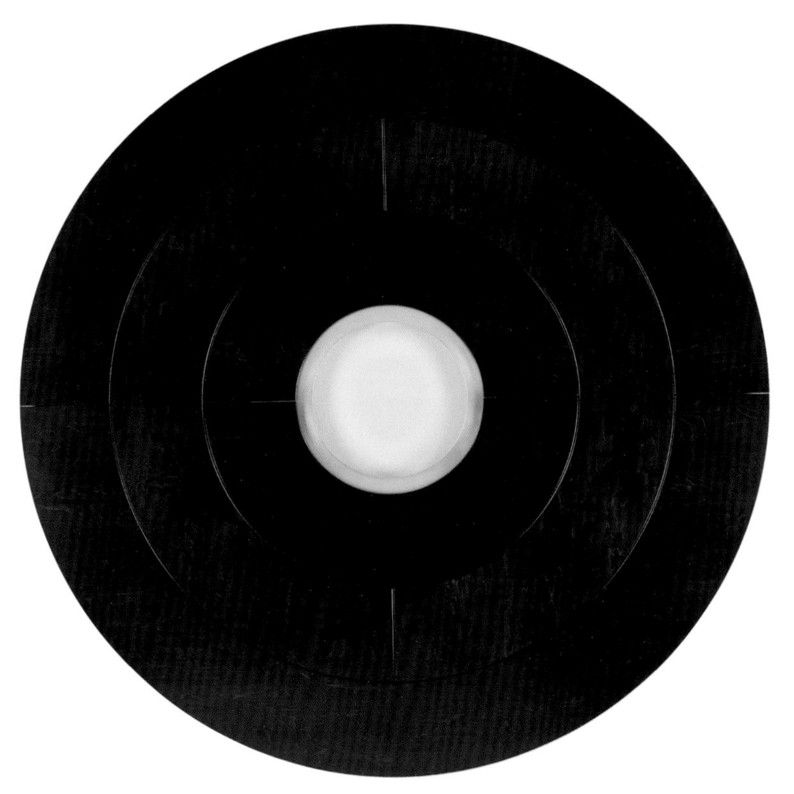

fig. 1

Sam Gilliam
Black Mozart/ORNETTE, 2020
wood, aluminum, die-stain, lacquer
96 × 96 × 2 ¼"

Fred Moten

The Circle With a Whole in the Middle

> The dye is transparent and shows the nature of the wood beneath, an aluminum ring in the center, very large; painting is a medium, he says; it's not just the work but the ideas that stimulate the work—Sudan, home of the early Masalit, African graves prior to Egyptian pyramids. Within that history a concept, a way of taking art as a form, not politicizing it but making it refer to other issues, so that part of the preparation is reading, the ideas, the painting as a register, the shapes, the whole of civilization that has been enslaved, to think of yourself as a part of all of humanity, an existence beyond the present. I have a friend who wrote, "Black is a Color."[1] Its reference is to whole content and not just the maker, a holistic thing. It says other things, transcends itself in terms of saying other things.[2]

I begin with a whorl of Sam Gilliam's words in order to let you know that the intent behind this writing is just a little bit more mimetic than analytic, but that's not my fault. Gilliam has drawn me in. I'm so attracted, and my absolute desire to have been attracted in no way militates against his attraction's strength. He makes work I can't get next to and can't get out of, and though I know I'm supposed to be writing something that you can get something out of, I want you to know that if you don't get anything out of it, it's not your fault. It's my fault, though it's all Gilliam's fault—his fault being more of a maelstrom, an irresistible whirlpool, whorl's absolute intra-action of depth and surface. If you don't try to get out of it, if you don't try to get anything out of it, you can be drawn in, too. You can hear when you're supposed to see and see what you're not supposed to. Passage from moment to moment, from material to material, may be swift and jarring. The spiraling continuity of Gilliam's career induces punctuated disequilibrium, a rush of steady contemplation, the apposition of the unthought, which turns out to have been thinking all along.[3]

Amiri Baraka hears, then hips us to, Ornette Coleman staving off bar lines, refusing their visual rule and carceral rhythm.[4] Measure, having refused unitary, sequential restrictions, becomes immeasurable or, more precisely, incalculable. What's at stake is not the absence but the animating irregularity of pulse. Wood, reed, blown, lets the beat, having been unstayed, wave and swing, waver and carouse. This is not meant reductively to suggest that in *Black Mozart/ORNETTE* (2020, fig. 1) Gilliam offers either a portrait of Coleman or a (re-)recording of his music. Instead what I insist is that they share the work of registration in which various practices of crumpled, twisted, blurred, burled, creased, stretched, stained material become communicable.[5]

This is about Gilliam's whorl-making: his voluminous, microtonal push and pull and grounding of color; his building and tenting and billowing of tint; his folding and sculpting of shade. Having seen through an open window the open secret of women hanging laundry, he set sail on quilted, common wind, in long, drawn-out circumnavigation. Where does he go with that? Where do we go with that? What does it mean to draw an artform out of lovely, deadly social information? Is something lost or found? Can nothing flee from loss and finding?

Black women's work is all but always watched and stolen, its status as work having never been given, the status of the work having been unsought except in individuation's shadow. The terror of enjoyment, the 'joying of one's freedom, are real and surreal abstractions for the women of Hot Springs or Atlanta or Soweto or Saint Louis or St. Louis or Washington, DC.[6] What do we make of what Gilliam makes of that? Art is a terrible, beautiful thing. The figure folds into the circle. It's not the figure but the movement of the circle. And if the circle implies matrilineal propulsion in the absence of the singularity, it also demands the ongoing socialization and ungendering and curled unfurling of matrilinearity—birth's dispersion and recycling are foregiven and unbroken in the circle with a hole in the middle.[7]

Not quite as free as the clothes they hang, black women hanging clothes out to dry (fig. 2)—and all but fly from being held or pinned in points of tension and then, in that arrest, ambivalently stand in for flying—can't not be seen as progenitors of Matisse's creased and Gee's Bent patterning. Caring for fabric teaches refusal of subjective, objectifying confrontation for good and ill in lateral, dorsal, worn attunement to what clothes us, which is all and nothing, all in nothing.
To wear and feel and wash and rub presages activation rather than enframing of wood or canvas. This surfacing bears an absolutely messy, absolutely precise aesthetic that wants to refuse art's

anti-sociality, its confinement, narrowing, and filtering in the mesh that's made of artwork, artist, and their institutions.

Black women's work resists Gilliam and resists through Gilliam, animating both his work and what his work resists. Insofar as he is dark as he is, Gilliam can't help but be an aesthetician of immense diversity. He can't help but be concerned with (the abolition of) the metaphysics of painting, bending it toward sculpture, folding it into music, letting it hang with performance so that in the coordination of his hand and our eye, painting is beside itself. Moreover, his paintings are gloriously beside themselves. But insofar as they are themselves, our concern must also be for the nature, structure, and life of their support. We want to think about how what's held in painting, which can't be saved by painting, can save painting for some common selflessness. When his drapes hang, you have to see who hangs them, the nonperformative force animating the studio, and then the gallery as a space of performance. The washerwomen remain in the folds as their very animation.

This or that Rembrandt is already an abstraction: the artwork is a monetary unit, always already leaving its materiality behind, as Theodor Adorno intimates, in the service of exchange, which is also given, and most fundamentally, not in the relay between the beholder and the beheld, but in that between the beholder and his own ideal interiority. The brutality we endure, which some are made to service, and others made to ornament, is given in that such exchange is inseparable from the way the painting is not just commodity but also financial instrument. The capacity to endure is given in the insistence with which we claim and live out service and ornament in the sensuality of the unseen, who are overseen, and the unheard, who are overheard; it is given in the thinking of the unthought, whose repression is brutality's constant study. The painting is not simply exchanged; it facilitates exchange, like the figure of the slave, which is also

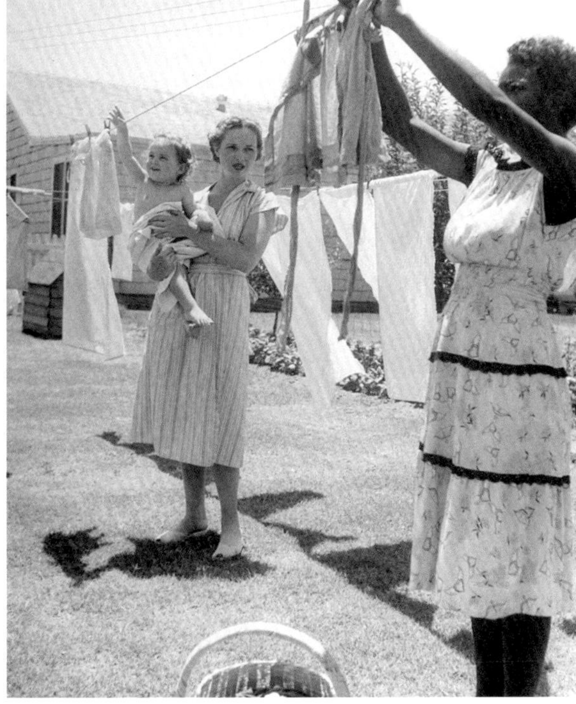

fig. 2
Nina Leen
A woman hanging the laundry out to dry, 1948

a real abstraction, held in the emission of an atmosphere, a world. But the animation of the painting, its folding out into the wind, is shared in the iteration of a whorl.

This contra(di)ction, which is the mystery Gilliam bears, is that which bears him and is that into which he is born. He draws us in there to consider with him and them the difference between sharing and exchange. What's the relationship between sharing and abstraction? Sharing, outside the logic of the equivalent, outside that accounting and accountability, is surreal abstraction, which doesn't so much recover but rather discloses lost materiality. Neither equal nor simply unequal "to the real itself," but a little past it or above it, below it and before it, a little south of it, hung, loose, ana-Lacanian but folded, fuzzy, eccentric, variously all but buried.[8] Finding is given through hesitation and refusal, in the no-thingness of the incalculable, which will have been extended in disclosure. I'm not trying to make an argument about some relation between Surrealism and abstraction. I do want to insist that the surreal abstraction disrupts the oppositionally unholy alliance of conceptualism and pictorial realism, each of which is submitted to portraiture, each of which is submitted to the elemental selfishness of art and its world and the endlessly reiterated manhood of its white mask, which looks back at the beholder every time. In this regard I am in love with the sound, the ana-monochromatic saturation, of Gilliam's black skein.[9] The whole in the middle of the circle is a dark landscape of need we share.

What if exchange always requires a medium? What if interiority or self-reflection or wonder or conviction are always also modes of exchange? This is what Clement Greenberg and his circle assume, and this is the ideological, metaphysical, and politico-economic structure both within and against which Gilliam operates, as black radicalism does the endless, open, choral women's work of fighting liberalism's interinanimation of slavery and freedom. Is he in the art world but not of it, as if on his own subversive, counter-ideological mission? Or is he (also) an activation, rather than an activist, of sharing the black and golden door through which we disappear? Consider the way that individuated things or collections of such things can be both medium and object of exchange. This is how art and artworks work now, and this working is especially sharp and problematic when the artworks in question are made by black folks who bear and enact the brutally quintessential performance of this interplay of mediation and trade, which is to say, of interplay, or relation, as such. The question concerning some other, less human and more humane modality of exchange is always raised, often with great beauty in black art and by black artists, and it is always also, and often quite gloriously, beside the point. About real abstraction and the irreducible brutality of relation, the old masters are never wrong.

Life—which turns, spins, spins out, whirls, whorls, unworlds, circles unbroken, centrepeats and centrifuges—refuses, avoids, falls out of the dead fall into equilibrium. And yet it feels like black life—its survivance, its sousveillance of the settler—has arrived. All this endless falling, and flying, comes to feel like standing, or standing's fantasy, which makes us want to stand, or take on standing's fantasy, or take some land to stand on, in order to regain some order, some needful, justified equilibrium (as Sylvia Wynter puts it in *Black Metamorphosis*, contrasting it with the settler's headlong neurotics of progress, which our falling, failing breath propels). And so, another paradox emerges: black bodies, who righteously seek rest, strain against black flesh's resistance of arrest. Arrival will have always been recuperative, always a reclamation not so much of what can't be had but of the fantasy of having, the capacity to own. But it's our dispossessed and dispossessive fallenness, our fallen mess, our fallingness, that keeps us alive, going, doing, moving, refusing, f(l)ighting, *meine lieblinge flüchtlinge*.

This paradox is terrible and beautiful and freaky. If there's a cure for it, I don't want it, but don't worry, there's no remedy for our displacement, our dis placement, our dis/place/meant. We can only turn in it, turn on it, and return to it.[10] There's no end to it. We are displacement's means. We aim to generalize—socialize—displacement, and what that means is not the closing but the sharing of our home unto its disappearance, on the one hand; not the aspiration for but evacuation of (the very idea of) home, on the other hand. These hands are open all the time, which is how we fight, which is how we give, which is how we live, which is our flight, and which is our fall through equilibrium. Gilliam's "first inclination was to run away from home," that impossible domesticity.[11] That inclination is handed by the mother, who expresses it in tense, convivial, sub-remembered surrepetitions of scrub, rinse, pin, release, and fold. His one hand/other hand circling in sewing, sowing, this spinning, spun out turning of tables, this washing, and watching, in being watched, is hers and works against certain logarithmic conveniences and algorithmic constraints. Afformative against the affordances of calculation, can the work be actually an-actuarial? Folded, somehow, into the folds it contains, out of a common wind that draping and folding and hanging bears, *Black Mozart/ORNETTE* isn't world picture but whorled, commensal platter, musical commensality, yardbird flown off the handle (there he go, look, here he come), the circle with a hold in the middle.

There's a homeless, itinerant, displaced monasticism—foregiven in an already begun beguine—that recursively animates Gilliam's work. A profane, prayerful gathering of approach and improvisational surfacing. A continual finding of (im)perfect ways. A futurial commonality recalled, his circling is his surfacing, steadfast in the practice of inventing what is to come, open in having been invented by what is to come, gently approaching what is to come as if it were already there, as if the artist might fall back through the quilting circle into washing, and hanging, without going or holding or being held at home. In the an-original light of something communal, of what can only be done communally, there is a continual practice of seeing through, which need not be limited or constrained or telescoped by the individual lens of the artist or the artwork. We can and must see through the communal registration of the communal as it is manifest or given in Gilliam, but we can see through even more in our practice, or renewed assembly and ceremony.

Gilliam could never be mistaken for an outsider, like Thornton Dial or the women of Gee's Bend or the women who do the laundry. Nor is he some opposing confirmation of that simplistic inside/outside split. It's not that he wasn't in the art world as much as he wasn't defined, and remains undefined by its real abstractions and inexistences, its metaphysical commitments. Here's where the palpable frustrations of Euro-philosophical criticality straining against its limits, the most fundamental of which is its comfort within its limits, becomes as sad as it is grating. But it's not just that or them, because black art's and black artist's claims in and

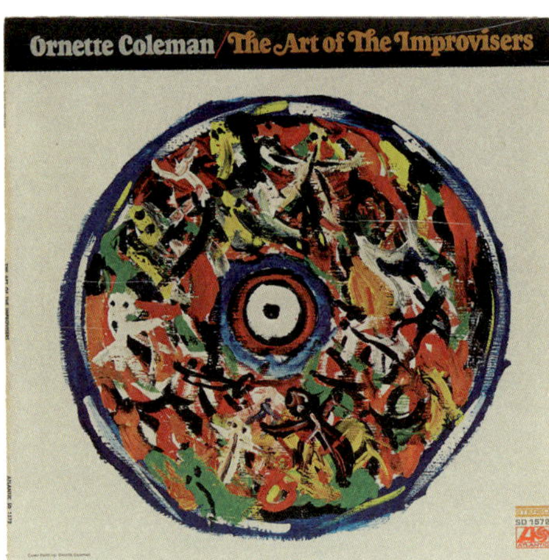

fig. 3
Ornette Coleman
The Art of the Improvisers, 1970

Courtesy Rhino Entertainment Company, a Warner Music Group Company

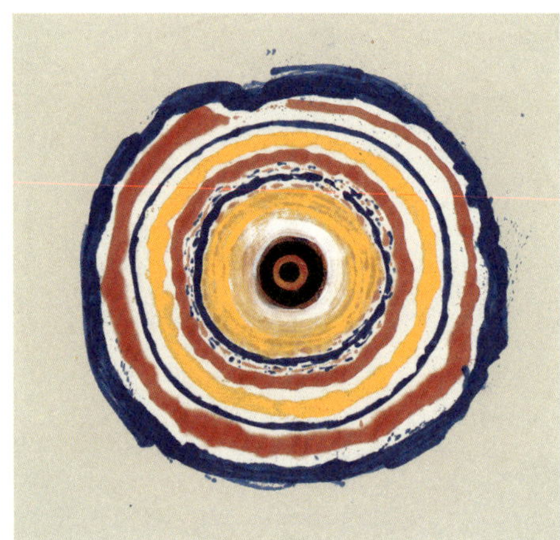

fig. 4
Kenneth Noland
Askew, 1958

Magna on canvas
67 ⅛ × 69"

© 2021 The Kenneth Noland Foundation / Licensed by VAGA at Artists Rights Society (ARS), NY

upon the art world are just as frustrated, just as frustrating, just as committed to the metaphysical foundations of the real abstractions they refuse. The surreal abstraction, in another sound Marx could only imagine as something he needed to imagine, is what Gilliam affords and that to which he surrenders. Knowledge of other dimensions, which spirals indicate; the incalculable rhythms and the wavering downbeat arcs; (sus)stained multitude and coiffured grain. What has it ever meant for a Gilliam to be bought and sold?

Coleman's 1970 album, *The Art of the Improvisers* (fig. 3), collects previously unreleased material recorded in 1959 and 1960, when Kenneth Noland was engaged in something like the working musician's serial experiments in recitation and repetition (figs. 4, 5). Surely the variations in color that were given in Noland's particular staging of a general experiment were matched night after night in the immersive discomposure to which Coleman submitted his compositions. Noland is concerned with the circle with the hole in the middle, but Coleman is not one of his unwanted followers. He's a fellow traveler gone askew, come out of nowhere, out of round and toward a clearing where broken chords and penitent clothes and schizophonic birds fly wheel in wheel through a black and golden circle.[12] Alma Thomas's circle (fig. 6).

Coleman's ornamental fury—his crowded, meticulous disorder, shades bourgeoning like bent, breathed, re-Traned sheets of sound—shares Gilliam's fierce impersonality, opening abstraction out past surreptitious portraiture, which exerts its force in the Cold War ideological impress of Abstract Expressionism as well as in the neoliberal market-driven, financialized discovery of heretofore overlooked and underviewed and overseen black abstractionists. They generate diagrams and sonograms of suffering, in all its wealth and poverty, through lovingly and brutally violent distributions and restrictions of gathering. The intraplay of data and lore in the turntables they prepare says maybe

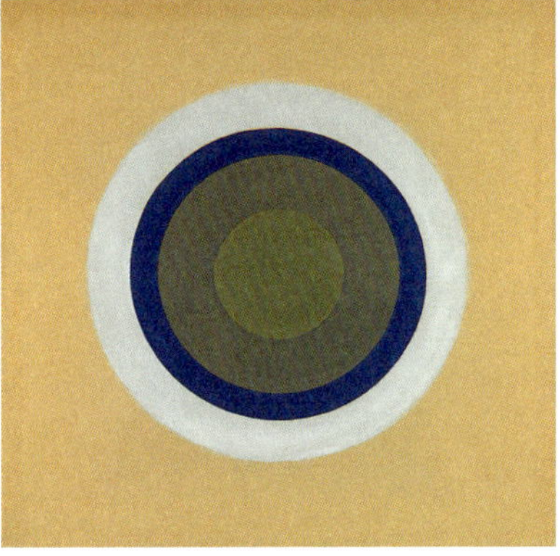

fig. 5
Kenneth Noland
Gift, 1961–62
acrylic on canvas, 72 × 72"

Tate, London. Presented by the artist through the American Federation of Arts 1966

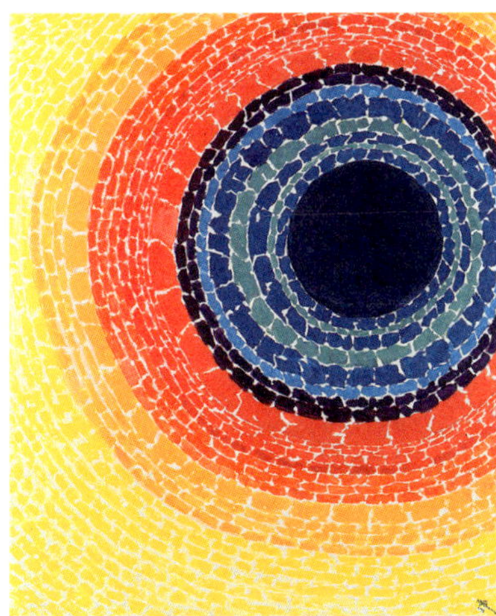

fig. 6
Alma Thomas
The Eclipse, 1970
acrylic on canvas, 62 × 49 3/4"

Smithsonian American Art Museum, Washington, DC. Gift of the artist

it's not that it's not portraiture but that portraits need not be personal. And if it's not about the round, recognizability of Rembrandt's face but the mystery of his hair, then we can ask, by way of the portrayal of the incalculable, after more than persona, mask, and real abstraction.[13] Not person but impersonation; impersonality in radical impersonarity; not voice but sound shared in the whorl. The ageless murmur of suffered, suffering, motherless, play-mothered children whirrs through the circle with a hole in the middle.[14]

Gilliam stays in the ecliptic circle of schoolteachers, which is a symphony of alms. There's *The Generation Below Them* (1989, fig. 7) and another deviant orbit, another coming around in bent unbrokenness. Not coming full circle, or the circle's eternal return, but the mobility Sterling Stuckey's embrace releases, the sweet homelessness of Henry Dumas's tangent, their work in the wake of women's work.[15] There were generations below, and before, and beside; some kind of turning out of circle, inside out, gone through, so that so-called flatness turns to side-eyed thickness, volume pierced from sun to air. Work, in its black(woman)ness, which was there and persists, and sustains through all the work, is to be seen through, and gone through, socially, as if it were open door, open secret, open home. What if there's nothing flat and post-painterly about it, if impasto is displaced in and by passion? What's happening in what we're going through? Gilliam's variant of soak-stain technique enhances grain, given in the absence of brushstroke, which induces an approach so much nearer and gentler that an anti-metaphysics is implied to trouble scale and cultivate environment.

A double problematic of absorption occurs when pigment, drawn into surface, builds volume not just out from but also through the plane, so that then the viewer is drawn in, as if open window had decided, after all, to rebel against mirror's dominance. *Aire*, or area, ensues. This extension of drawing draws you in, as singularities are said to do, but there's a whole, not a one, a whorl, not a world in the middle, whose earthly incompleteness we share in having been drawn through portraiture, as presencing, in promenade. The improvision of this listening walk is Charlie's and Billy's and Cherry's and Ornette's, or Nate's, with dusty angels pulled endlessly through doors of no return, mapping ongoing non-returning, choreographic and chorographic and phonographic and holographic in the shared writing of the dis/place/meant.[16]

Noland was always submitting strict geometry to movement and being moved. His circles became increasingly flirtatious with the perfection they'd once fled in color bleeding out of line with seismic motivation. His gifts of simplicity, turning, turning, trying to come round right in wheelwright repetition, keep showing a way from which Gilliam faithfully deviates a half-century ago, and again last year, in what he calls "the draperies' elongated figure."[17] Now, his black

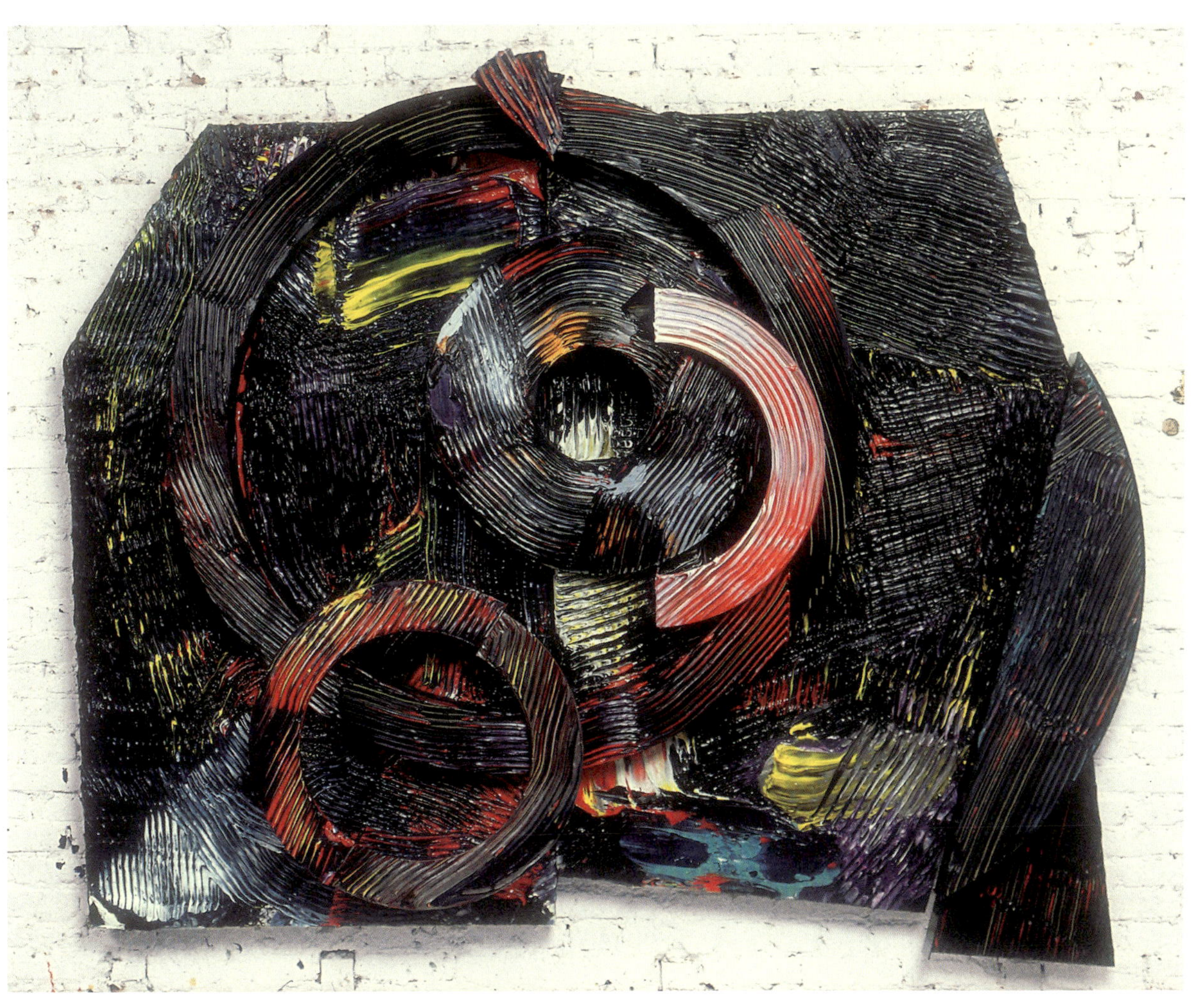

fig. 7

Sam Gilliam
The Generation Below Them, 1989

acrylic on canvas and primed
aluminum with plywood structure
80 × 96 × 13"

waves of grain show precise aberrance and discomposition. The soaked and stained was already rich with black, transbluescent worry; the wood has its own version of the drama that is foregiven in and by Gilliam's canvases, which are social fabric.

To sustain is sculptural, environmental; but it is also to fall, to spiral. Conspiratorially, the circle's shared breathing bears both flying off the handle and tending toward decay. Thrown off, drawn in, disequilibrium is centrifugal and centripetal, too, tending toward a center that is not there and an outside that's in here in all this bending in and out toward nothing either way. Gilliam approaches a complicity, in and through the work, which works through him, that ecologically undoes the work of art. Rough in being wrought and going through, in being brought through being bought, collage, in subtraction of the center, moves in recessive surfacing, out into the whole. In Gilliam's taking of a turn through his black paintings, his focal point has, at its heart, the absence of a focal point, which induces gathering and common presencing.[18]

There, the particulars having given way to nothing, surreal until they are observed as merely probable, a field or smoke of this or that, abstraction pierces and refreshes observation. Look for you today and here you come yesterday is the difference between evident rhythm and incalculable rhythm, the death rate and the women's club, in all its beautifully spooky, nonlocal incompleteness. It's hard to find what had not been lost but held, then blown. That matter, that information, that indiscretion, the babbling gossip of the air, the area, the territory, the terrible beauty, is a record, a surface, which keeps on spinning. Then why assume that information, which can't be lost, comes in discrete units? Why continually accede to the very idea of the discrete unit? It's as if what Leonard Susskind calls the "negative-first" law of physics, that information can't be lost, assumes a law of metaphysical accounting, namely, that what is can only come alone. Metaphysical discretion keeps coming back, *even in physics*, no matter how much physics keeps exceeding it in falling short of it.

But physics won't stop breaking the metaphysical law, especially when black washerwomen and black musicians and black painters and black schoolteachers steal it back from Dutch mastery. They teach us how not to accede to the denial of anticipatorily disunifying excess and deprivation. They say entanglement is a refusal, and not a fusion, of such discretion. They share a practice, they till a field, of indiscretion. If we want to study where accretion troubles discretion, where we accede to an-original excess, we have to look so closely at the grain of wood that it begins to flow in the wind like liquefactive clothes.

The volume that drawing determines is drawn out into area, horizontally, cryptographically, under duress, in caressive whisper. What's not particular very carefully and insistently and selflessly rubs up on itself in surfacing—richly, and with great profundity, refusing to go into an assumed, proposed interior. If real abstraction in the history of painting, which is the merger of the concept and the portrait, shines the numerical light that lets the particle and its awesome interiority emerge, then the surreal abstraction registers and releases disorder, entropy, the refusal of the transfer of energy into (the) mechanical work. This disorder, this open secret energy, this little all but general strike can't be calculated as a set of definable variables that might be called degrees, or agents, of freedom.

Entropy is pan-African revolt, which is swarm, not solo; social, not political; aesthetic, not artistic. Bobby, I don't know; but whatsonever I play, it's got to be funky: like an old batch of collard greens or some smothered steak or some mobile gumbo or some mumbo jumbo or some callaloo or pulau, *un poco loco* in our dispersive focus on sanity. Some madmen came up with a genocidal experiment to prove we can't happen and the experiment just made us happen differently. And so, the difference between observation and surrealization breaks down where what doesn't get lost just disappears. Susskind asks, "What is the proper dimension of a world that is bigger than our cosmic horizon? Is our cosmic horizon just a two-dimensional scrambled hologram of all that lies beyond it?"[19] Raymond Saunders replies, black, which is a color, worldlessly registers the scramble (the hot bit soup that has no bits, the muck, the terry, the whatsonever, the surreal presence neither here nor there nor now, hownever, Nevèrÿon).[20]

Endlessly self-absorptively, the white register *wants to* register its own three-dimensional emergence as if it were a flourishing rather than a reduction. There's no world that's bigger than our cosmic horizon. There's no accounting for the making of signs and the taking of hands, but what continues to emerge is the black and turning surface of our two-dimensional entanglement against the rise of single three-dimensionality. There, in the still mobility of the performative studio, Gilliam and Coleman share dis/place/meant's nonlocal indigeneity—black and blue and incomplete and an-autochthonous. They share the nonperformance of laundry, which laundresses share, which is not theirs, which was not theirs.

This double-double redoubledness of Gilliam and Coleman, of *Double Merge* (*Carousel II* and *Swing*; 1968) and *Black Mozart/ORNETTE*, that I keep trying to put together, in which those who do not count and are incalculable are not lost but disappear for all to see, is what I can't help but see and hear, here, where I'm dancing in your head. The titles indicate varieties of troubled proximity within a general concern for how stuff goes together, which is a sociological and aesthetic—rather than metaphysical or traditionally ethical or ontological or artistic—question. Consider what it is to play one note, or write one word, or make one mark or stain and then to add another (worried) note or (troubled) word or (folded) stain, which feels or sounds or looks good or blue or right, next to it. But not right next to it: there's a seriality that can't be straight or uninterrupted; a proximity, or approximity, that's all up in and not just next to, so that even the (very idea of the) one (word or note or stain), with which or as which one begins, withstands no scrutiny.

Consider the foregiven complicity and complexity of "I Can't Get Next to You," which is the theme song of common presencing in the focal point's dispersion.[21] What if what, and that, we share makes you and I unbearable? Consider the unbearable beauty of "my life is incomplete and I'm so blue/'cause I..."; and "Unhappy am I, with all the powers I possess/'cause girl, you're the key to my happiness, and I..."; while noting that "I" is falsified and unraveled by Dennis Edwards and Eddie Kendricks, cutting and augmenting each other past the point of undoing, unbridgeably distant from "you," who fades away into y'all, y'all, when we're dancing out of our heads. Does the serially para-consecutive disrupt art's executive functioning? At the same time, and in the same place, can that which follows with, or follows from, also be with and also be before, and before, in ecstatic co-presencing? This folds into questions concerning the practices and protocols of empathy, embrace, solidarity, approach, surfacing, suffering, and foregivenness. Are sight and sound grammars, or a set of radically un- or ana- or holo-grammaticalities, implied and required? In order to investigate and ornament, Gilliam joins various practices of anti- and ante-metaphysical experiment.

It's not that Gilliam isn't fully immersed and in love in the history of painting. It's just that he's uncomfortable in it, is discomfiture in it, at restlessness in and out of it, and in and out of others' estimations or misunderstandings of his dis/place/meant in it, of it, having fought and fled its metaphysical supports, in spite of its invasive centering. Immersion and being in love is differing. He's not in between painting and sculpture. He's dancing in the collective head, awash, a washerman, not in between Helen Frankenthaler's name and black women's washing's almsful all-but-namelessness. Pan-medial, ana-medial, animaterial, he's appositional in and to that history and its erasures. Off in them, off to the side in them, or of them, or in some ante-black churchical derangement of in and of and off and out so that the spatial arrangements of category in (art) history are submitted to seismographic, topographic disruption. The wayward ways he keeps finding are not his but shared in an absolute differentiation that can be seen in terms of both the assertion and the constant striation of his singularity. Gilliam is foregiven to the making of ways. He makes ways and waves in and through his own history, turning in it, turning on it, elongating and crumpling it, merging it and creasing it with rough-dried, air-dried, absolute beauty.

> From several things I was thinking about doing in 1968. Then my first notions were verbal, as opposed to being acted upon. I'd seen Al Held; I'd seen Stella; I'd seen shape—what we'd call erratic shape. I'd seen Barney Newmans; I'd seen Pollocks. *Blue Poles* was sort of a reference. I'd been painting stripes and doing this very, very hard-edged thing—getting into Albers' interaction and working very logically with masking tape and striping. But I realized that ideas I was dealing with were mostly someone else's. But the prelude in pre-industrial art, from which these guys' ideas came, was also in my mind...what was most personal to me were the things I saw in my own environment—such as clotheslines filled with clothes with so much weight that they had to be propped up.... That was a pertinent clue.[22]

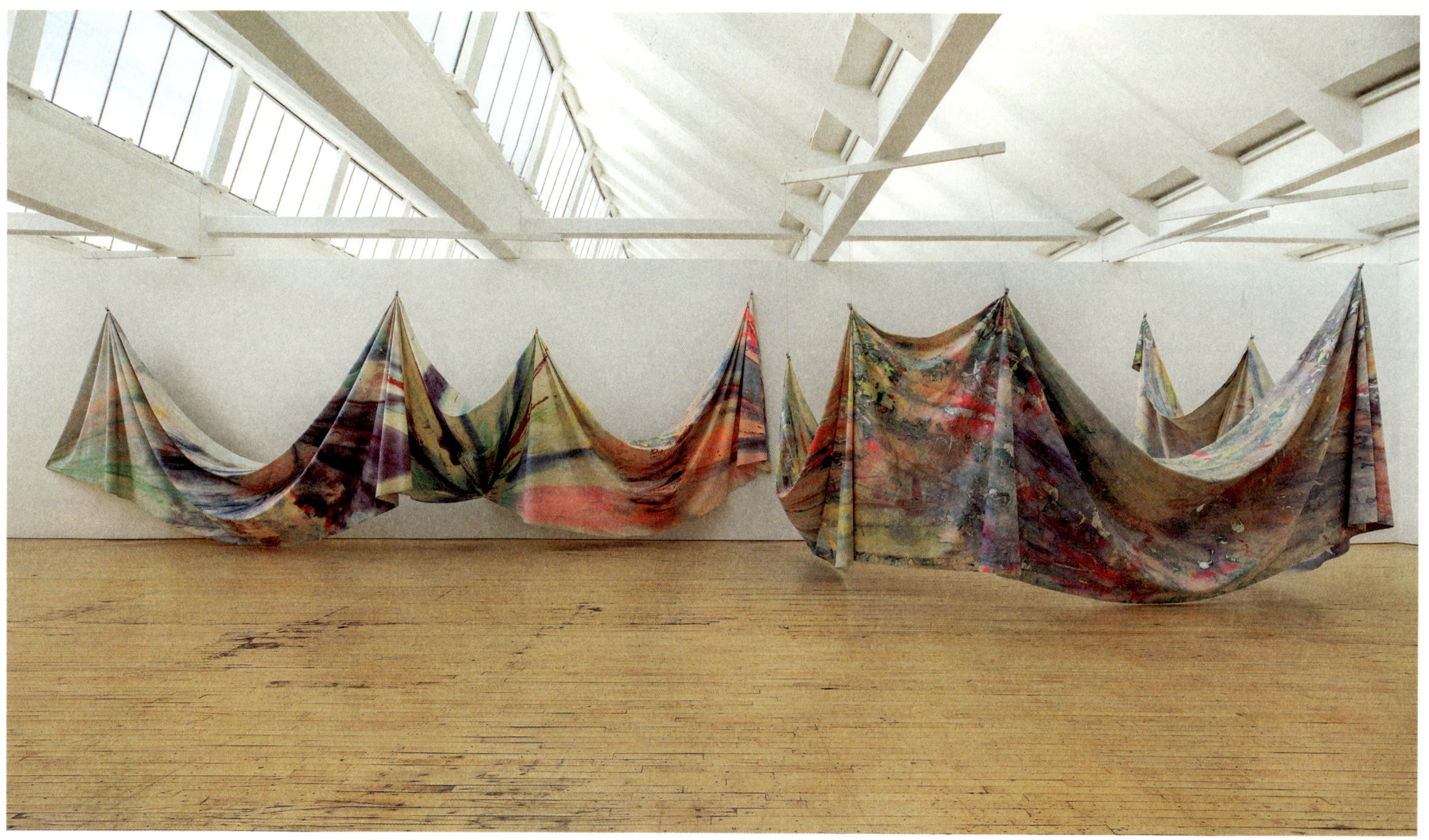

fig. 8
Sam Gilliam
Double Merge, 1968
Installation view, Dia: Beacon, New York, 2019

At the installation of Gilliam's *Double Merge* (figs. 8, 9), I went looking for a preview of *Black Mozart/ORNETTE*'s wood-whorled grain. He makes it so we can almost go up in there before we see it from outside. We get to all but go through it. Surfacing, we approach as if in exodus. It's as if there always were these movements of and toward and through what Hélio Oiticica gives in the name of *Penetrables*, where striding into color and its theory lets us see where we've been walking all along. For about as long as it took to play "Doughnuts" in my head, I made a slow tangent with *Double Merge*, as if in some imaginary third volume of *At the Golden Circle*.[23]

It was this hunch that I would find (the) late work in the early work, as a detail, a small whorl, a fuzz ball, a juke joint, a missionary room, the surrealistic spot. But I realized at *Double Merge* and in it that they were a magnificent, animated detail in *Black Mozart/ORNETTE*, magnified and partially released, in anticipation of their thickened, hardened, mobile concentration. The drapes are the grain of the wood, the richness and depth and non-flatness of its surface. Gilliam

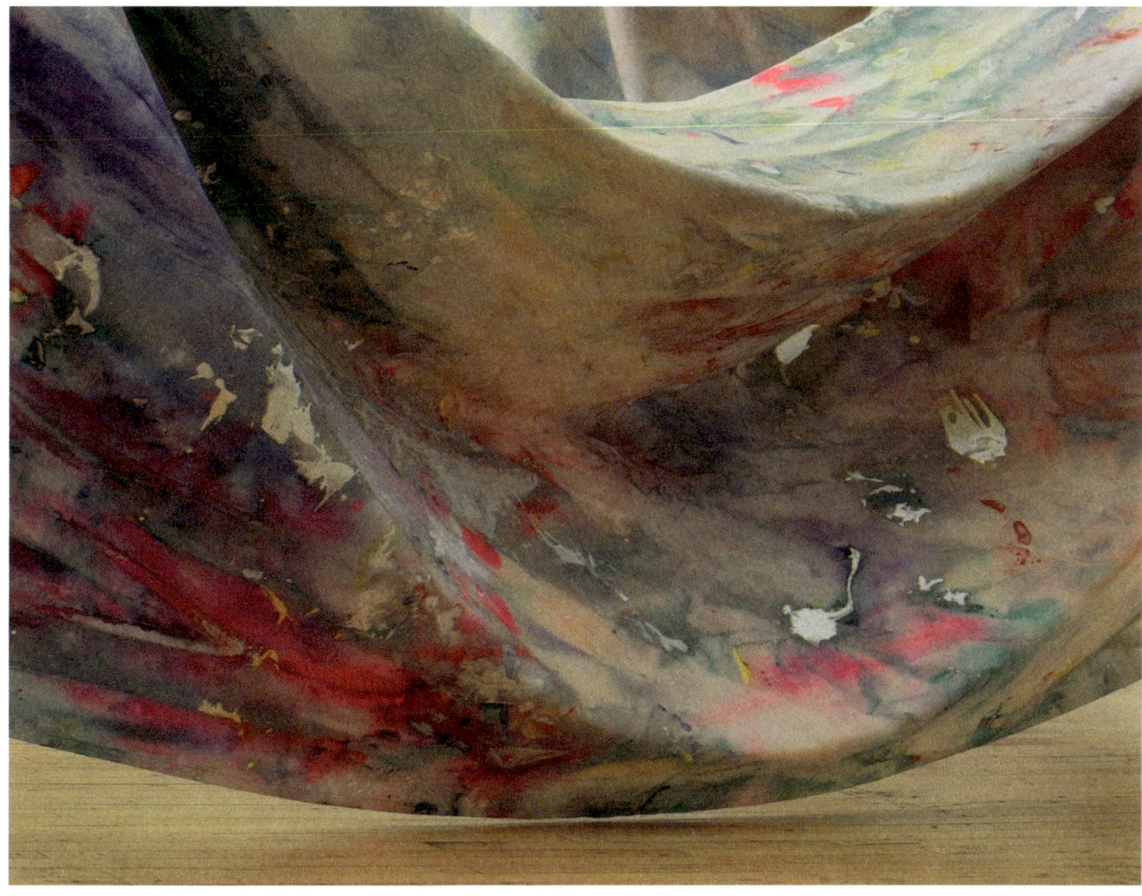

fig. 9
Sam Gilliam
Double Merge, 1968
detail

gives us a sense of the holograph we walk around in by letting us walk around in it, hastening and facilitating and softening our approach while messing time up, too. Because if *Double Merge* is old and new, from both 1968 and 2019, so then is *Black Mozart/ORNETTE* both new and old, 68, 20, bearing and reversing and extending the never-ending year of our lord and our bond and our refusal of lordship and bondage.

What is it to groove with Ornette's circles and ornaments? Does melody ornament pulse in a complex of irregularities encircling and entangling the line, the string, as it turns, building field? Is this that intraplay of plain (plain song's infinite extension of line) and (polyphonic/polyrhythmic) field, of orbiting run amok, orbiting ingrained, whorl upon handed whorl? Melodic line ain't straight; it drapes and folds and volume is produced and disappears as we move from plane to plain to polyphony in this long, swarmed duet. What if we're just details of one another, in one another, things only to have been seen as effects, only to have been surrealized as affects,

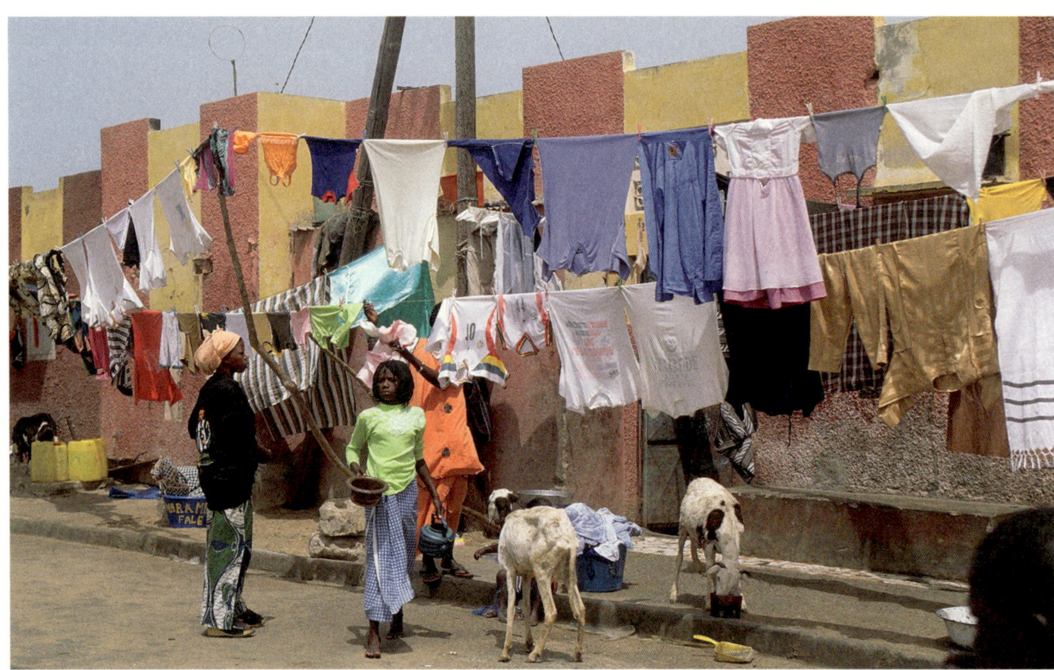

fig. 10
Wet clothes hanging in street, Langue de Barbarie, Saint Louis, Senegal, West Africa, 2006

as the radiant information of a fall, a way, a way in and out of the opposition of in and out. A maelstrom born of ana-cosmologically redoubled merging, *Carousel II* and *Swing* seem to come through a door to one another, each beside itself beside the other, redoubled, reemerged. And *Black Mozart/ORNETTE* is the non-singularity in and to which they are drawn: a gathering of presence, not that which arranged the rendezvous but rendezvous' an-arrangement in mind's, in boundary's, dissolution.

What does *and* look like? Is it *in's* familiar or internal flaw (its held, fallen, throwing eccentricity)? What if we (want to) say there's something all up in the swing of reiteration, of the daily, of impossible domesticity's windblown retro-speculation? Asymptotic, adductive in abduction, this beautiful merger of emergent moments is the refusal of touch that we call touch, which is touch's anti-metaphysical opting out of one and two: as in when we touch, we are not touching because we were never separate; as in touch is always only felt repulsion, the force of difference that animates all drawing in, all this long and longing fall and work in folding, this whorl we go through, this washing (fig. 10), colors' push-and-pull refusals of support, all that strike and strife and terror and enjoyment, all that animaterial schooling, information not lost but held in all that beauty, what happened, something happened to us, nothingness happens with us, the circle with the whole in the middle.[24]

1. Raymond Saunders, "Black Is a Color" (1967), in Darby English, 1971: *A Year in the Life of Color* (Chicago: University of Chicago Press, 2016), 266–75.

2. The words in this prose block were recorded by hand and then remixed, from my telephone interview of Sam Gilliam, conducted July 14, 2020.

3. "The Position of the Unthought: An Interview with Saidiya V. Hartman Conducted by Frank B. Wilderson, III," *Qui Parle* 13, no. 2 (Spring/Summer 2003): 183–201.

4. LeRoi Jones (Amiri Baraka), *Black Music* (New York: William Morrow & Company, 1968).

5. Tendayi Sithole, *The Black Register* (Cambridge: Polity Press, 2020).

6. Saidiya Hartman, *Scenes of Subjection* (Oxford: Oxford University Press, 1997); Tera Hunter, *To 'Joy My Freedom: Southern Black Women's Lives and Labors after the Civil War* (Cambridge, MA: Harvard University Press, 1998); idem, "Atlanta Washerwomen's Strike" (1881), in *Encyclopedia of U.S. Labor and Working-Class History* Vol. 1, ed. Eric Arnesen (New York: Routledge, 2007); Alberto Toscano, "The Open Secret of Real Abstraction," and Marina Vishmidt, "Speculation in a Sense: Aesthetics and Real Abstraction," in *In the Mind but Not from There: Real Abstraction and Contemporary Art*, ed. Gean Moreno (London: Verso, 2019), 17–41, 109–20.

7. Ornette Coleman, "The Circle with a Hole in the Middle," *The Art of the Improvisors*, Atlantic 1572, 1970; Robert Palmer, "Ornette Coleman and the Circle with a Hole in the Middle," *The Atlantic*, December 1972, https://www.theatlantic.com/magazine/archive/1972/12/ornette-coleman-and-the-circle-with-a-hole-in-the-middle/305870/. Accessed June 27, 2020.

8. Charles Olson, "Equal, That is, to the Real Itself," in *Collected Prose*, ed. Donald Allen and Benjamin Friedlander (Berkeley: University of California Press, 1997), 120–25.

9. Frantz Fanon, *Black Skin, White Masks*, trans. Richard Philcox (New York: Grove Press, 2005); Clyde R. Taylor, *The Mask of Art: Breaking the Aesthetic Contract—Film and Literature* (Bloomington: Indiana University Press, 1998).

10. Aimé Césaire, *Cahiers d'un retour au pays natal* (Paris: Presence Africaine, 1939/2000); Amiri Baraka, "The Return of the Native," in *SOS: Poems 1961–2013* (New York: Grove Press, 2014), 147–48; M. NourbeSe Philip, "Dis Place—The Space Between," in *A Genealogy of Resistance* (Toronto: The Mercury Press, 1997), 74–112.

11. Sam Gilliam and Hans Ulrich Obrist in conversation, in this volume, p. 38.

12. Ornette Coleman, "Embraceable You," *This Is Our Music*, Atlantic SD 1353, 1961; Franketienne, *L'Ouiseau Schizophone* (Paris: Éditions Jean-Michel Place, 1998); "Insularity and Internationalism: An Interview with Kaiama L. Glover," *Public Archive*, June 4, 2013, https://thepublicarchive.com/?p=3881. Accessed May 3, 2018.

13. W. E. B. Du Bois, "Sociology Hesitant," *boundary* 2 27, no. 3 (Fall 2000): 37–44; Whitney Battle-Baptiste and Britt Russert, eds., *W. E. B. Du Bois's Data Portraits: Visualizing Black America, The Color Line at the Turn of the Twentieth Century* (New York: Princeton Architectural Press, 2018).

14. Ornette Coleman, "Embraceable You," *This Is Our Music*, Atlantic SD 1353, 1961; Franketienne, *L'Ouiseau Schizophone* (Paris: Éditions Jean-Michel Place, 1998); "Insularity and Internationalism: An Interview with Kaiama L. Glover," Public Archive, June 4, 2013, https://thepublicarchive.com/?p=3881. Accessed May 3, 2018.

15. Sterling Stuckey, "Introduction: Slavery and the Circle of Culture," in *Slave Culture: Nationalist Theory and the Foundations of Black America* (Oxford: Oxford University Press, 1987), 3–97; Henry Dumas, "Will the Circle be Unbroken," in *Goodbye, Sweetwater: New and Selected Stories*, ed. Eugene Redmond (New York: Thunder's Mouth Press, 1988), 85–91; Christina Sharpe, *In the Wake: On Blackness and Being* (Durham: Duke University Press, 2016).

16. Nathaniel Mackey, *From a Broken Bottle Traces of Perfume Still Emanate, Volumes 1–3* (New York: New Directions, 2010); Dionne Brand, *A Map to the Door of No Return* (Toronto: Vintage Canada, 2001); Walter Benjamin, "On the Concept of History," in *Walter Benjamin: Selected Writings, Volume 4, 1938–40*, trans. Harry Zohn, Howard Eiland, and Michael W. Jennings (Cambridge, MA: Harvard University Press, 2003), 389–400.

17. "Sam Gilliam with Tom McGlynn," *Brooklyn Rail*, September 2019, https://brooklynrail.org/2019/09/art/sam. Accessed May 9, 2020.

18. In "Oral History Interview with Sam Gilliam, 1989 Nov. 4–11," he says: "And in the black paintings, later, of 1977, coming back to painting, I started to work with the center, started to work with a kind of a surface that was both surface and recessive at the same time." Archives of American Art, https://www.aaa.si.edu/collections/interviews/oral-history-interview-sam-gilliam-11472. Accessed May 9, 2020.

19. Leonard Susskind, "The World as a Hologram," arXiv, September 28, 1994, https://arxiv.org/abs/hep-th/9409089. Accessed, February 19, 2020; "Leonard Susskind on the World As Hologram," YouTube, November 4, 2011, https://www.youtube.com/watch?v=2DIl3Hfh9tY&list=FLImvk9REXzx6AmX6m2bW03g&index=29.

20. Saunders, "Black Is a Color," 266–75; James Brown, "Make it Funky," Polydor: PD 2-14088, 1971; Samuel R. Delany, *Return to Neveryóna, or: The Tale of Signs and Cities—Some Informal Remarks Towards the Modular Calculus, Part Four* (Middletown: Wesleyan University Press, 1994).

21. The Temptations, "I Can't Get Next to You," *Puzzle People*, Gordy GS 949, 1969.

22. Donald Miller, "Hanging Loose: An Interview with Sam Gilliam," *ARTnews*, January 1973, https://www.artnews.com/art-news/retrospective/archives-interview-sam-gilliam-1973-10735/. Accessed July 22, 2020.

23. The Ornette Coleman Trio, *At the Golden Circle* Volumes 1 and 2, Blue Note 7243 5 35518 2 7; 7243 5 35519 2 6, 1966.

24. James Baldwin, *The Fire Next Time* (New York: Dial Press, 1963); Wilderson, *Incognegro: A Memoir of Exile and Apartheid* (Durham: Duke University Press, 2015).

I would like to express my gratitude to Maxine Gordon, for her assistance and friendship.

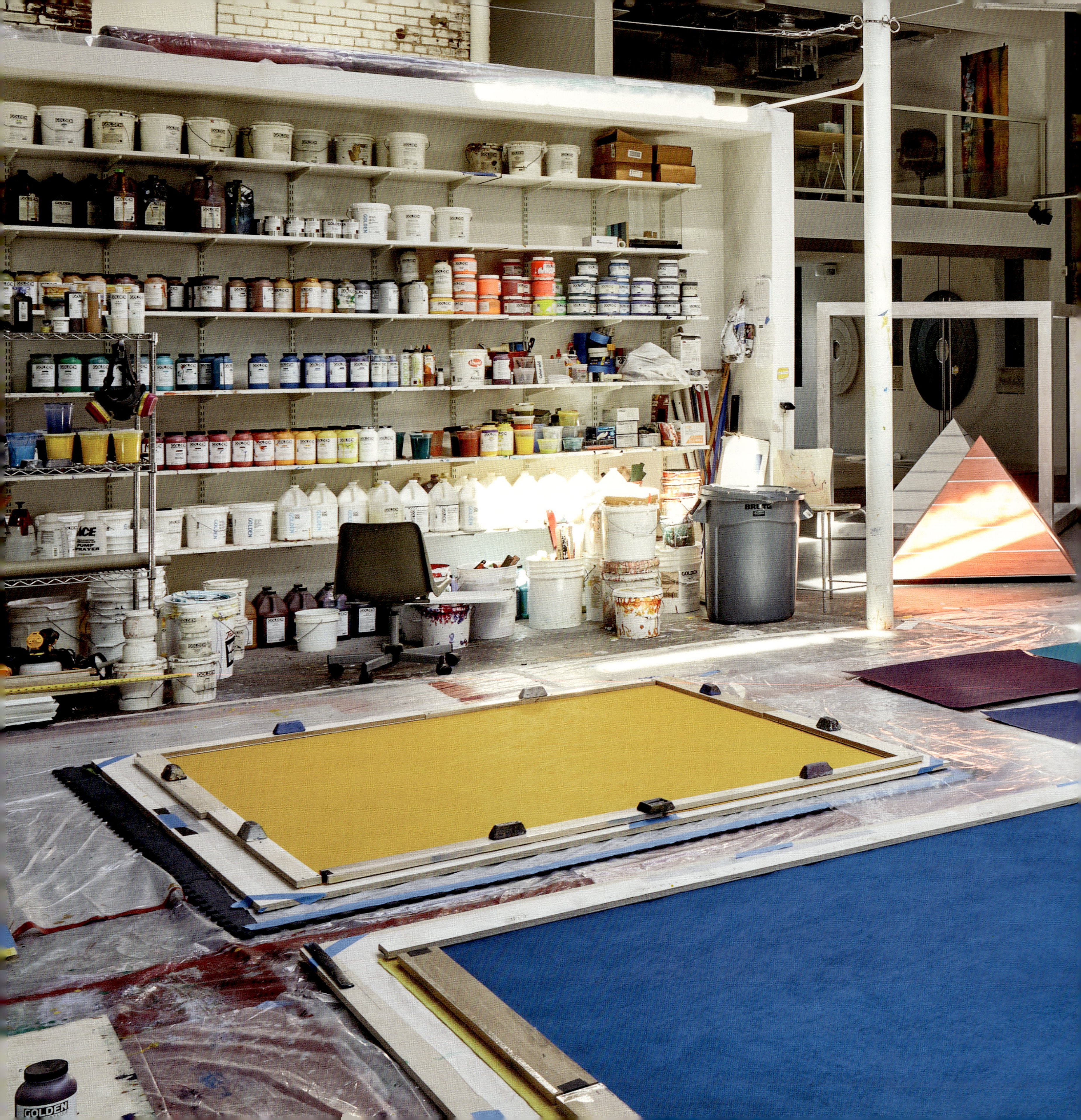
ACE
GOLDEN

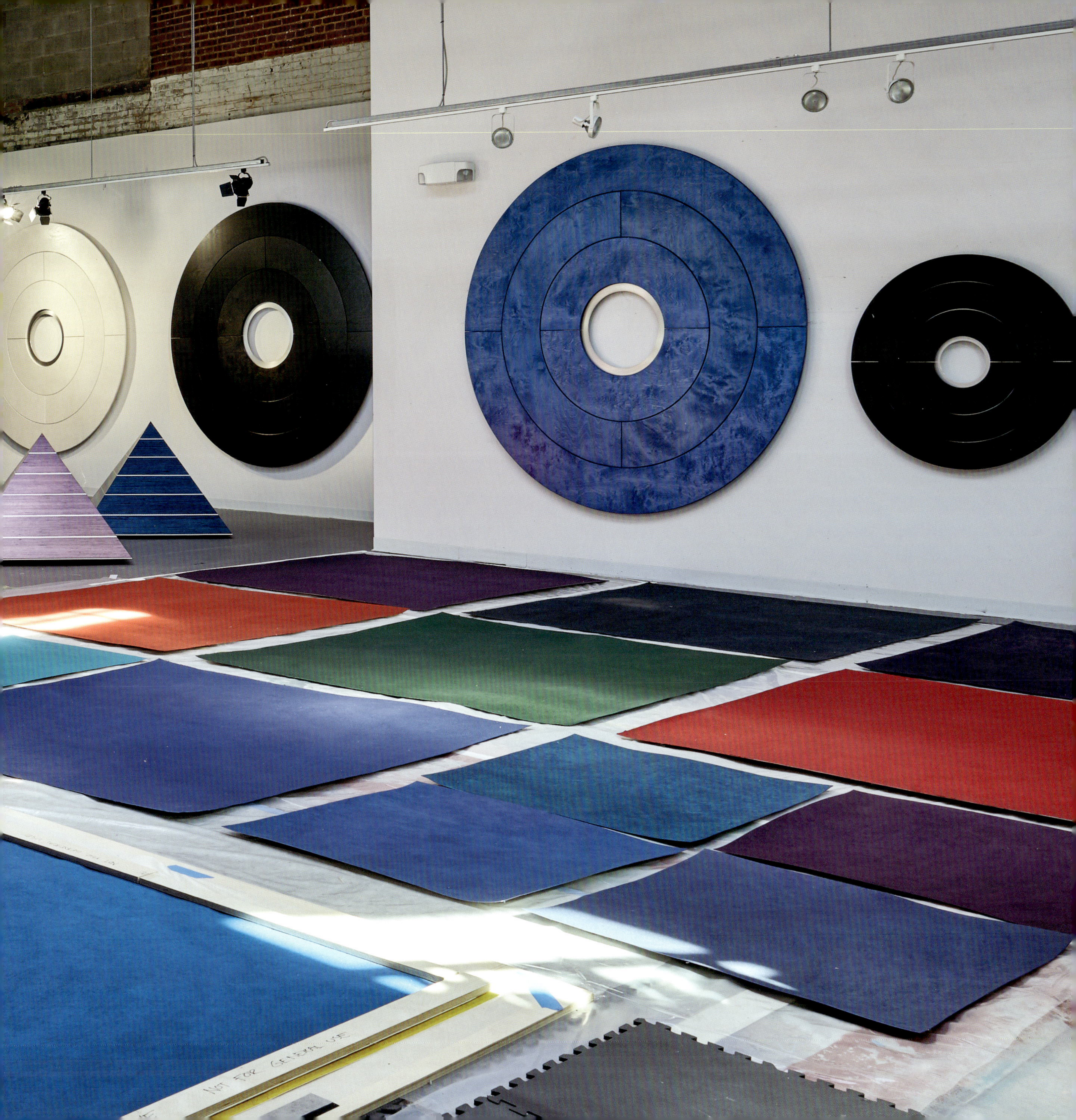
NOT FOR GENERAL USE

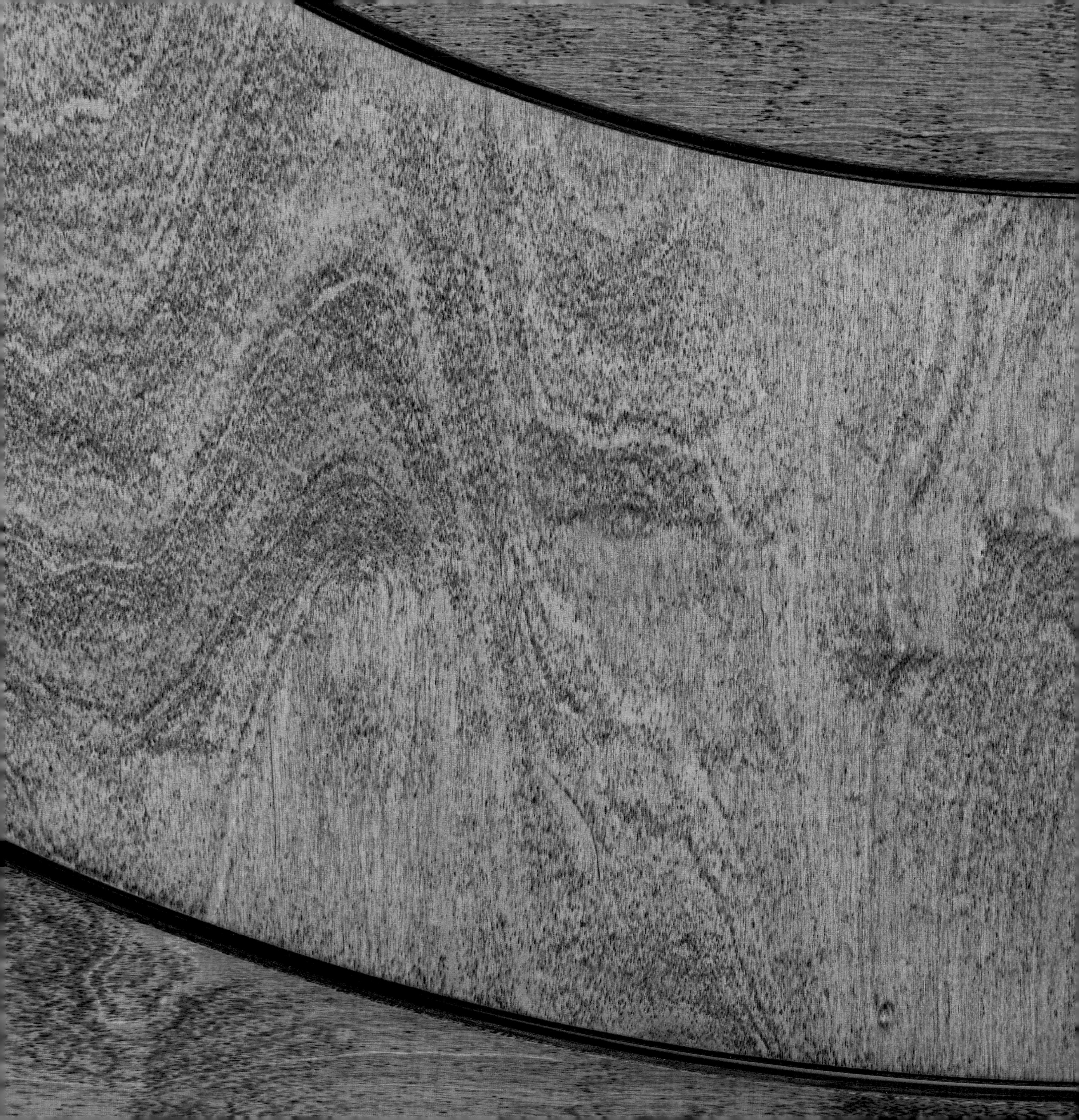

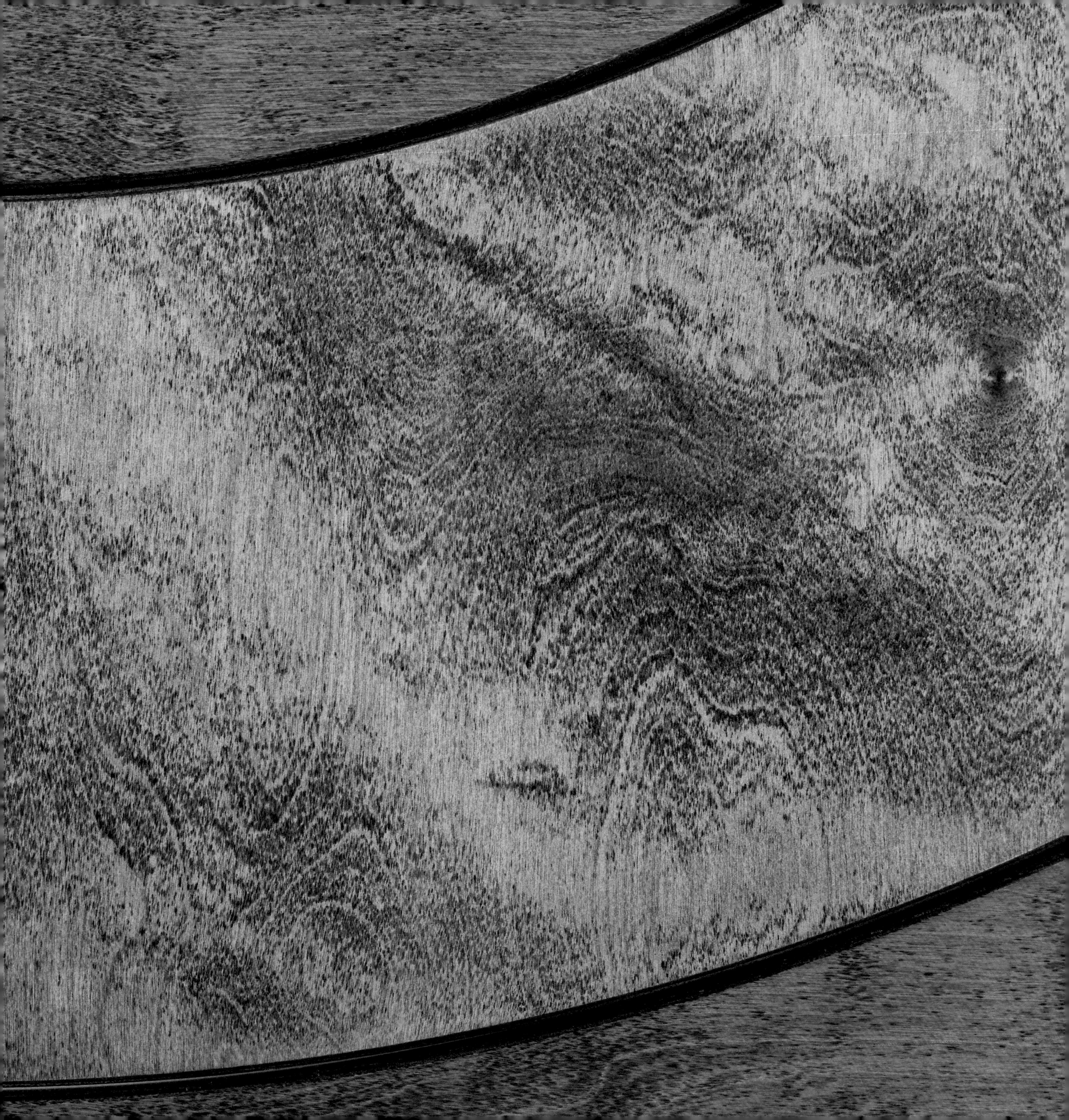

Blue 96" Disc | 2020 | wood, aluminum, die-stain, lacquer, 96 × 96 × 2 ¼"

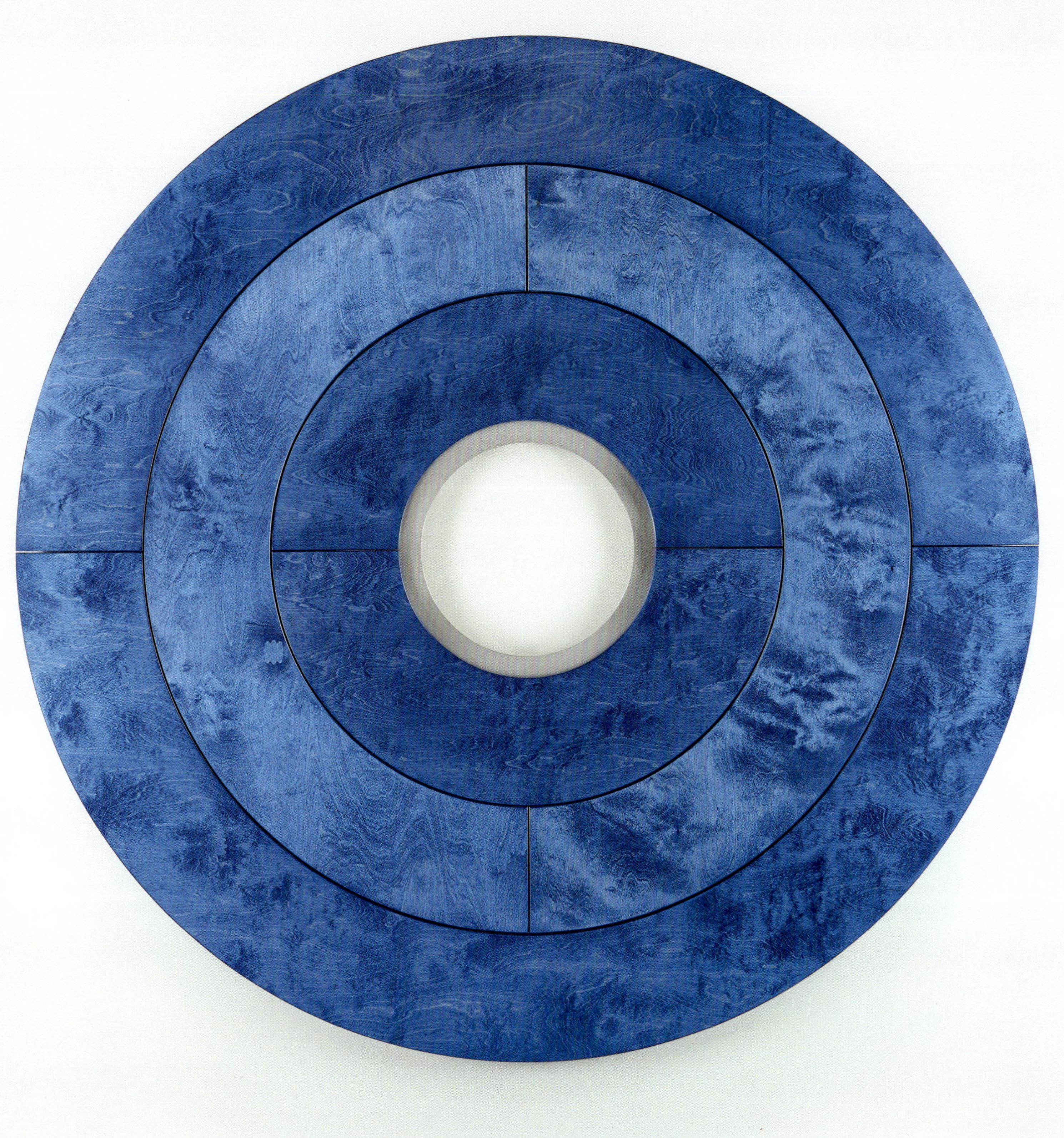

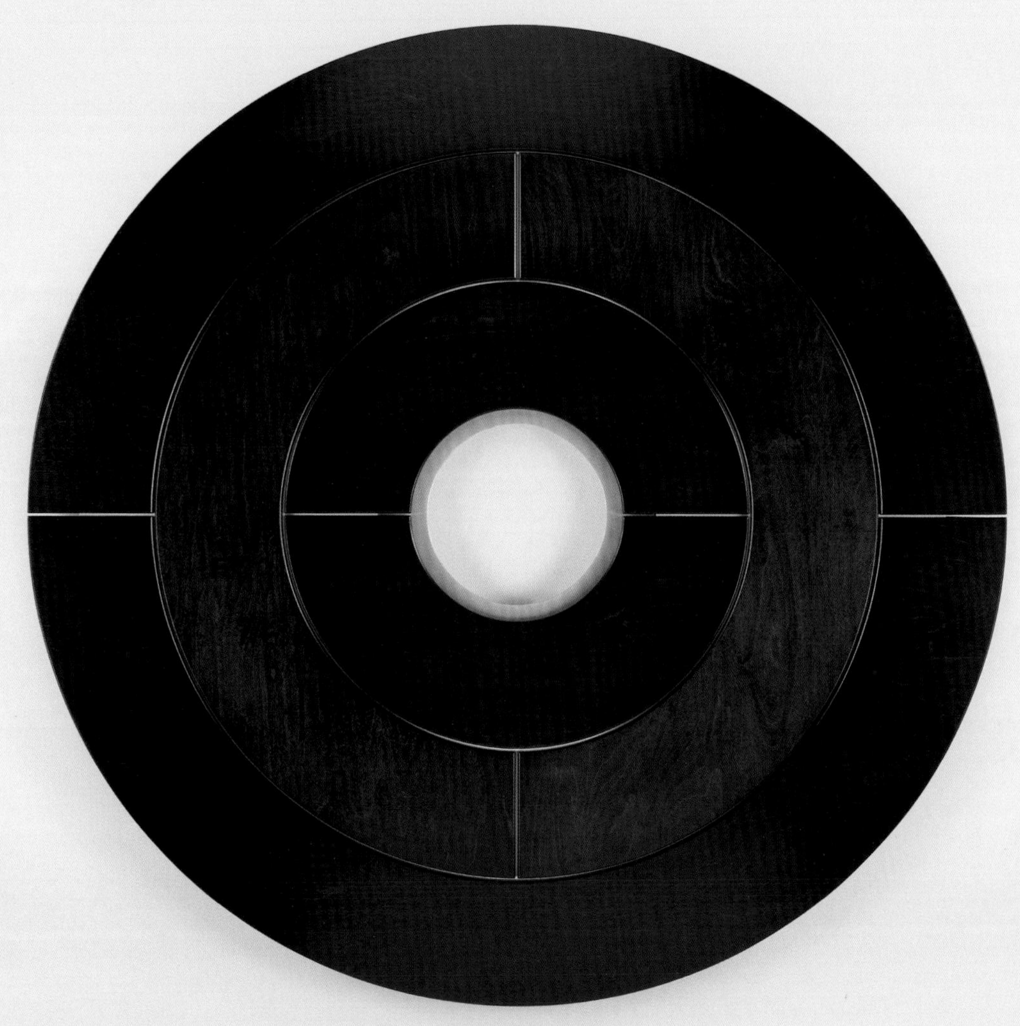

Black 60" Disc | 2020 | wood, aluminum, die-stain, lacquer, 60 × 60 × 2 ¼" | variant 1 of 3

White 96" Disc | 2020 | wood, aluminum, die-stain, lacquer, 96 × 96 × 2 ¼"

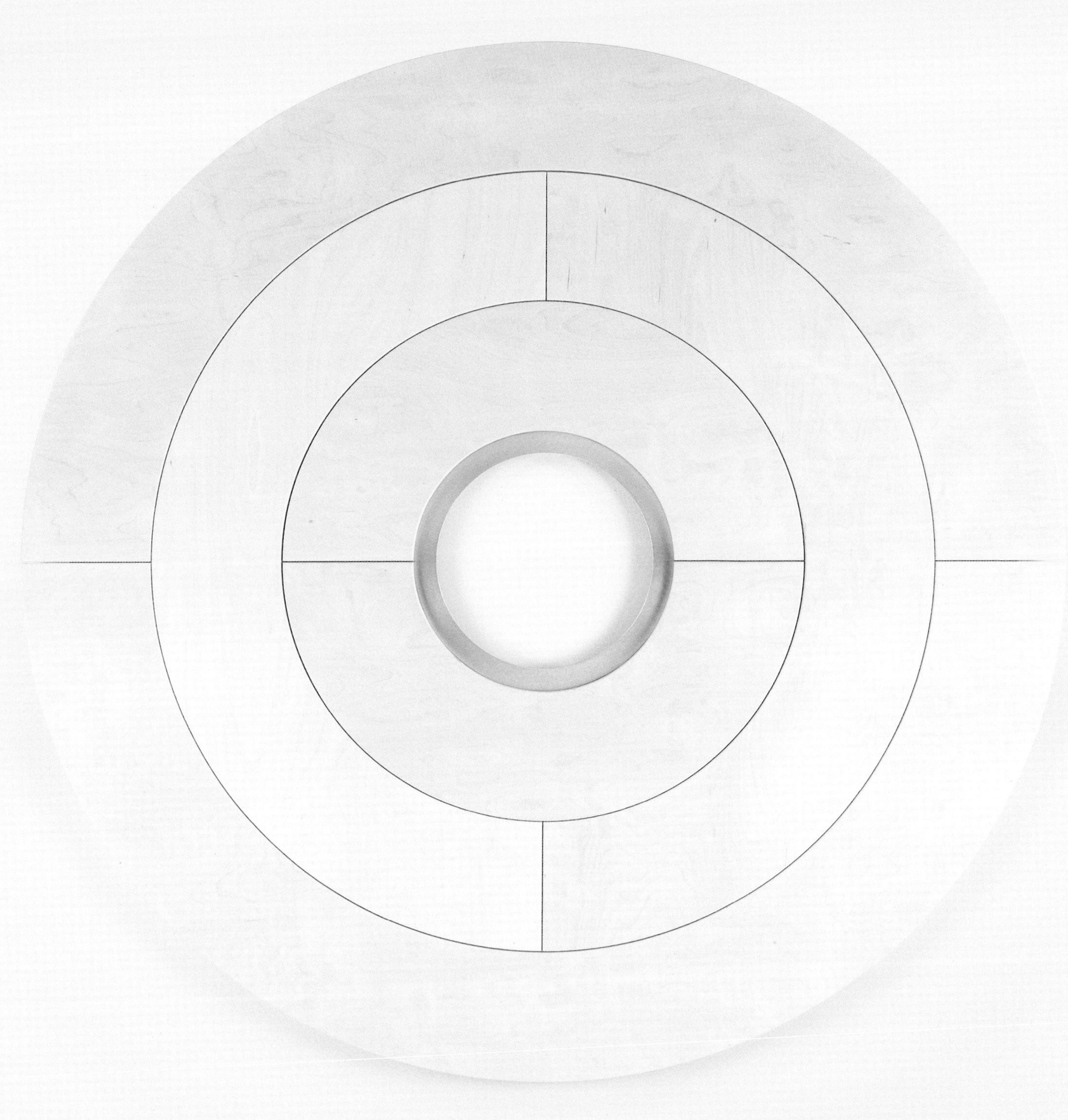

Black Mozart/ ORNETTE | 2020 | wood, aluminum, die-stain, lacquer, 96 × 96 × 2 ¼"

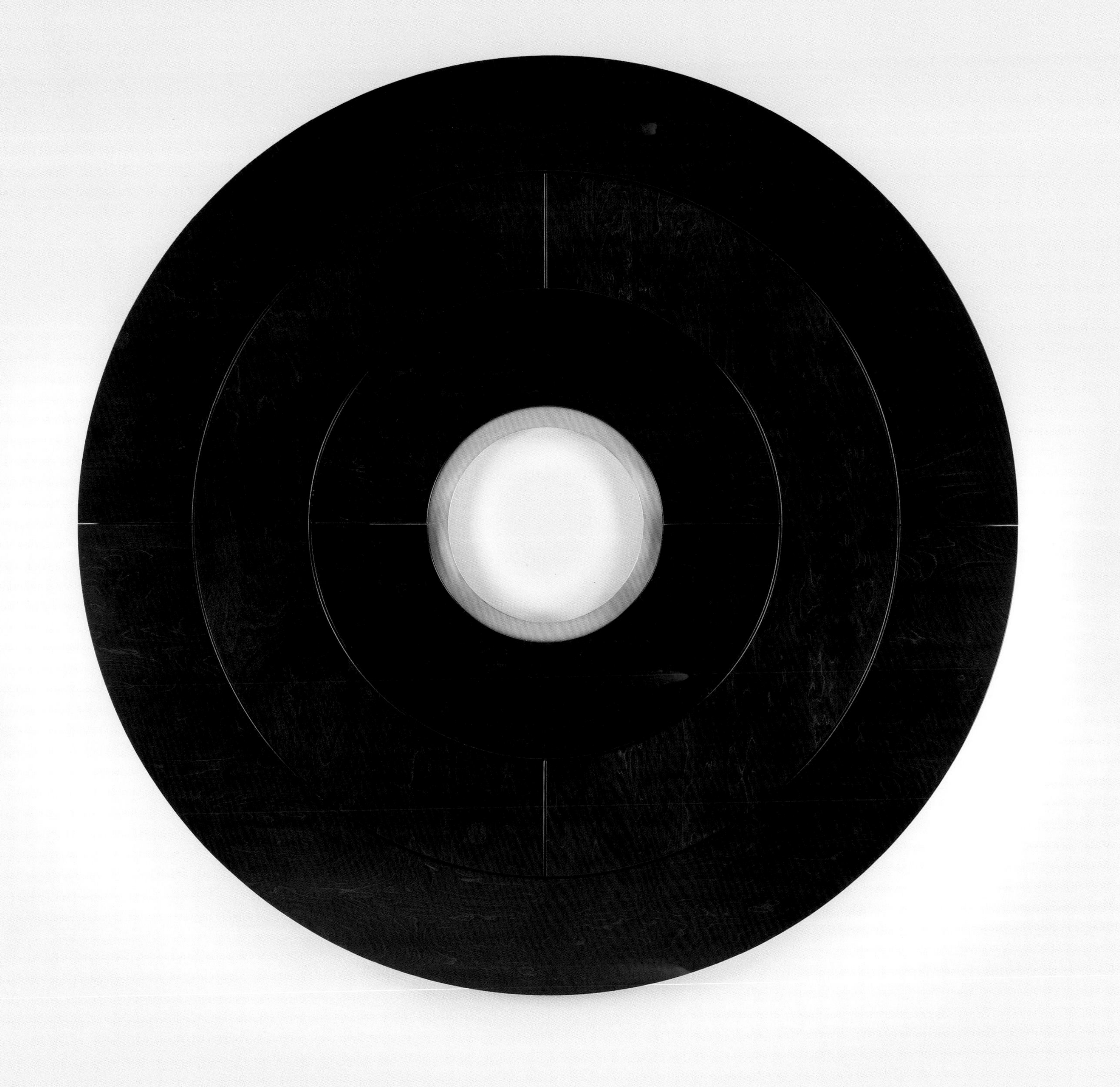

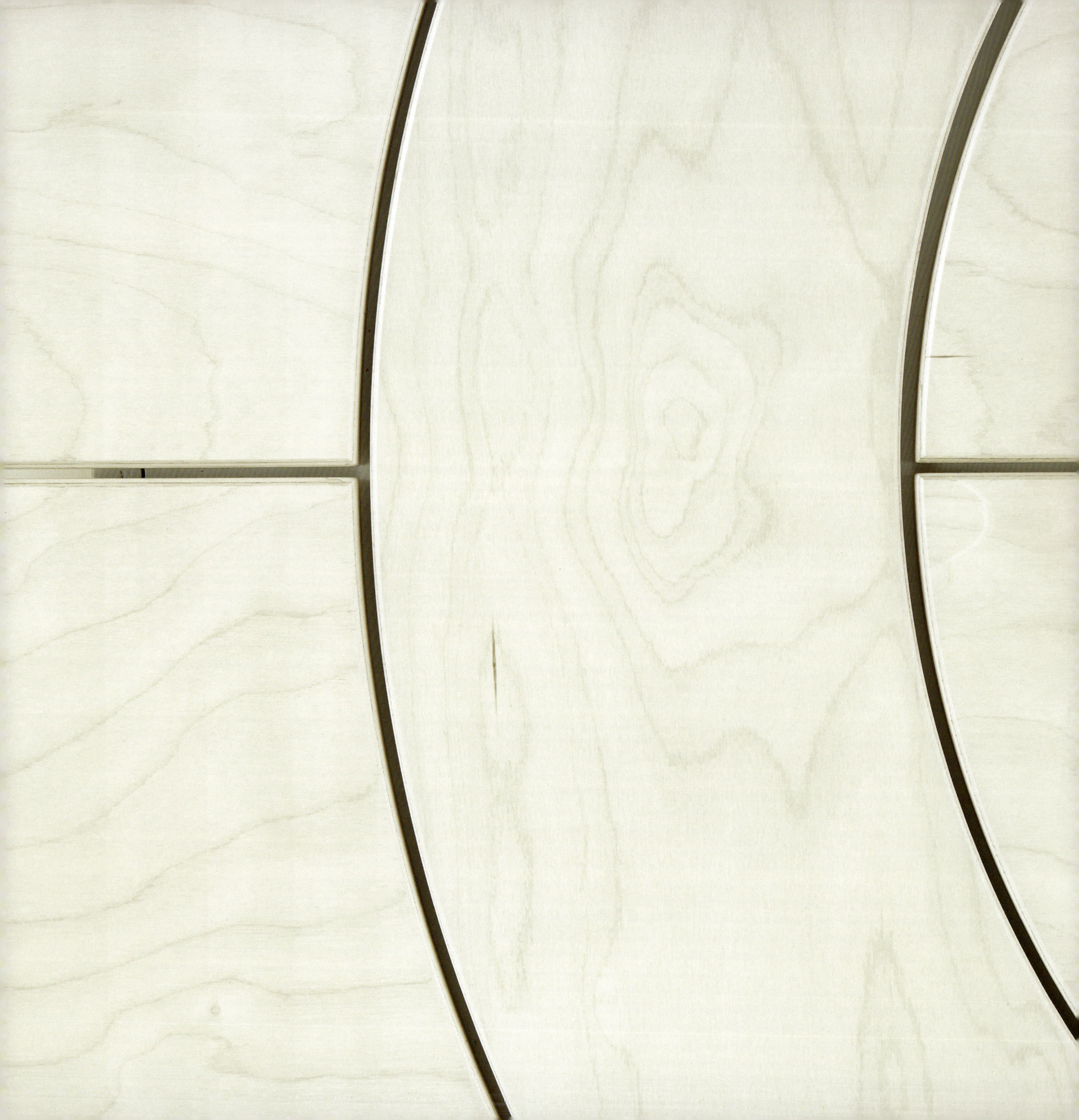

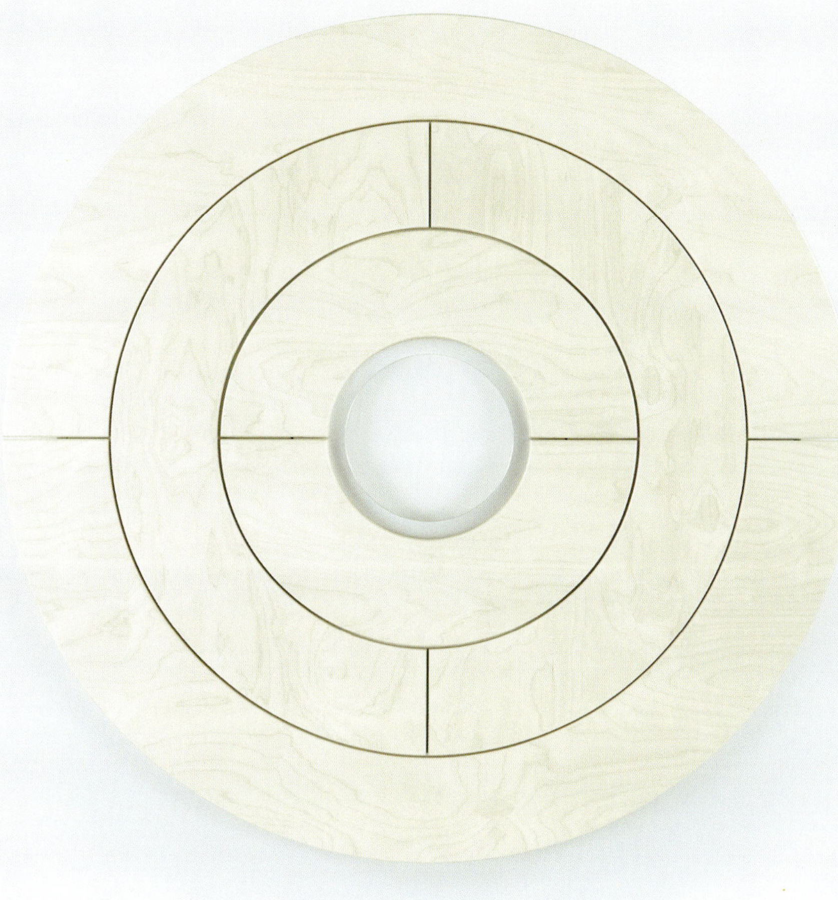

White 48" Disc | 2020 | wood, aluminum, die-stain, lacquer, 48 × 48 × 2 ¼" | variant 1 of 4

Black 48" Square | 2020 | wood, aluminum, die-stain, lacquer, 48 × 48 × 2 ¼" | variant 1 of 8

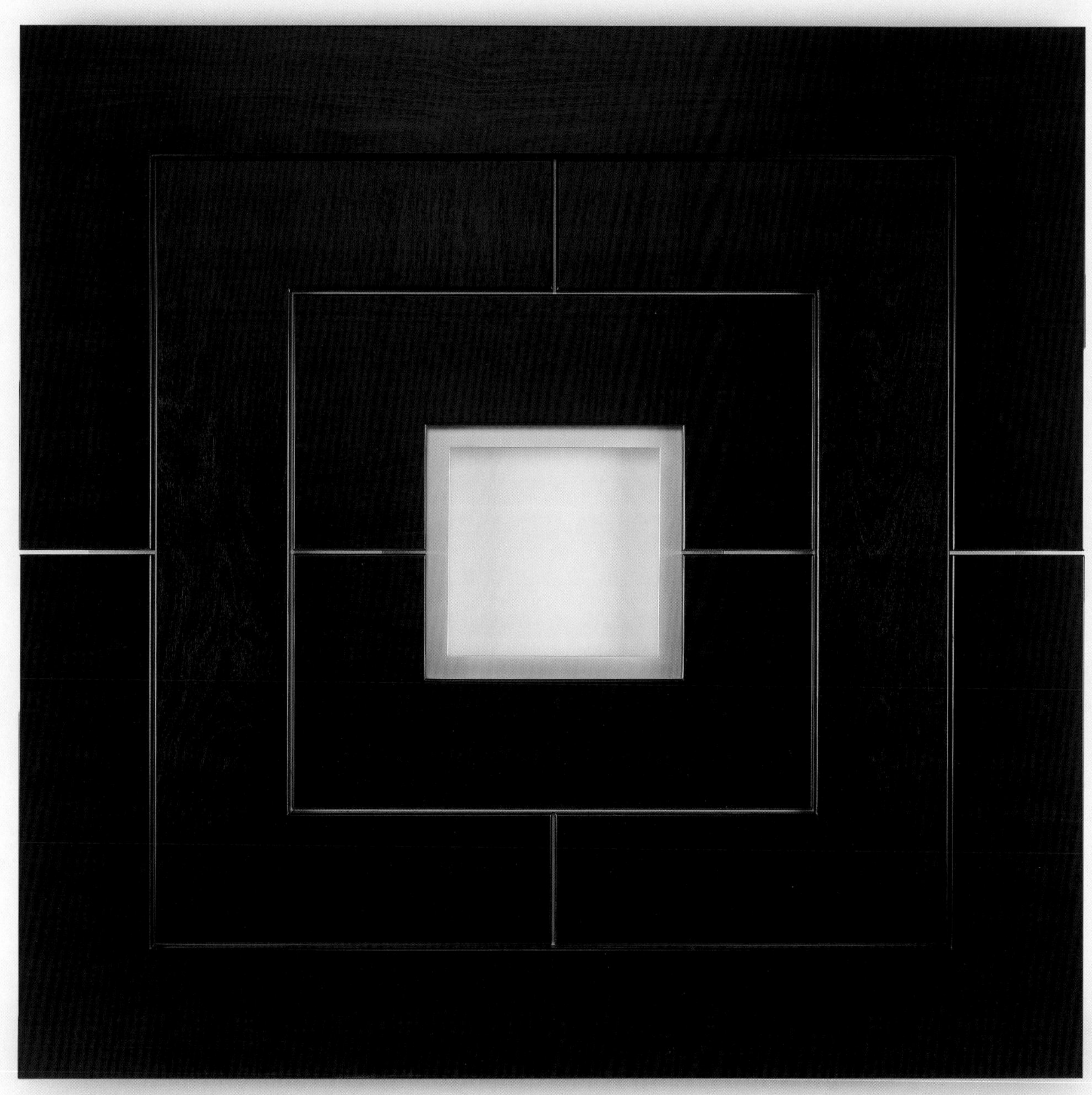

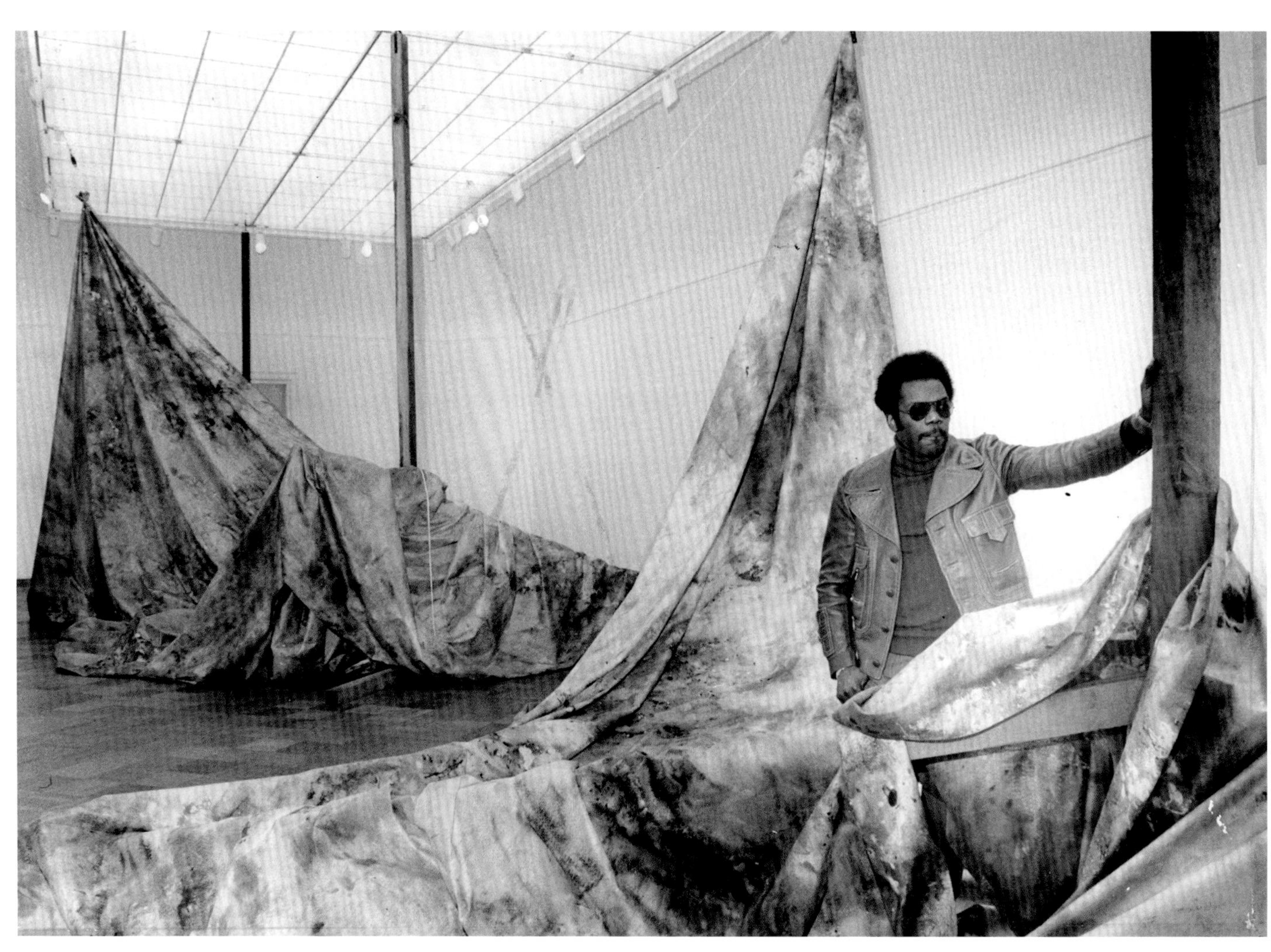

fig. 1

Sam Gilliam
Autumn Surf, 1973

Installation view of
Works in Space, San Francisco
Museum of Modern Art,
February 9–April 8, 1973

Courtney J. Martin

Imagine the Show on the First Day

Works in Spaces

In 1973 Sam Gilliam's work was included in a group show at the San Francisco Museum of Art (now the San Francisco Museum of Modern Art) titled *Works in Spaces*.[1] Unleashed from the museological parlance of "galleries," various areas of the museum were conceptually re-designated as free-form, architectural environments where the ceilings, extant walls, fixtures, floors, and passageways could be used or ignored at the discretion of the artist. Of the five artists whose installations were on view (Stephen Antonakos, Ronald Bladen, Gilliam, Robert Irwin, and Dorothea Rockburne), all had explored the space between mediums (Rockburne through dance and painting, and Bladen by way of sculpture, for example), which was a direct influence of earlier Abstract-Expressionist painters and their contemporaries in Minimalism. While the exhibition's goal may have been dialogue, the show resulted in singular statements by each artist. This was especially true for Gilliam, who, after one of the other artists maneuvered their work closer to Irwin's, ended up with the most enclosed or clearly defined gallery room. This allowed him to expand his large-scale draped painting *Autumn Surf* (1973, fig. 1) to the full contours of the architecture. Perhaps unknown to the curator and certainly not to the artist, whose tenacity gave him a better location, Gilliam's display-making ethos was predicated on responding to the space once in situ. His process, then and now, is syncretic:

> You begin to imagine the show on the first day. I try not to arrive at a concept of it in advance. Sometimes you dream about it at night. You live with an uncertain moment, only to arrive at the end.[2]

Gilliam's conclusion found *Autumn Surf* hung from several points in the ceiling before dropping down to the floor. Oriented along one of the room's long walls, it extended out from one of the short walls to make a convex bay that visitors could walk into (toward the wall but not totally around) or alongside. Parts of the solid length of polypropylene canvas were lapped over wooden bars constructed as right-angle arms to standing wood columns that ran from floor to ceiling. The armature under the drapery allowed for a series of formal cloth protuberances throughout the room, some distinguishable as elongated isosceles triangles. The draping was Baroque in its fluidity, and the room was an undulating territory, with an overall effect that was an immersive, flowing, painterly balance between elegance and crudeness. From either end of the gallery, viewers could take in the peaks and valleys of the material and its dense, rich color, achieved by the repeated soaking and staining process that he had mastered, and for which he was, by then, well known.

What Gilliam achieved in *Autumn Surf* was the culmination of years of problem-solving complex equations with which he tasked his art. From the early 1960s he added a number of technical changes to his process that affected how he worked and the ways that his works were received. In 1965 he began to paint without a stretcher. By the next year he poured paint directly onto unprimed and unstretched canvas. In many of these compositions he made use of beveled-edge stretcher frames, which created significant depth to an otherwise two-dimensional form by adding in a forty-five-degree angle (either facing toward or away from the wall) to all sides. By 1968 he suspended swaths of canvas from varying heights or draped them over industrial implements, including ladders, two-by-fours, and sawhorses. The juxtaposition of high-key color, an excess of unprimed, unstretched canvas, and construction elements was high and low, rough and refined, unwieldy and yet totally harmonious.

Within a decade he had moved from the late Abstract Expressionism that permeated his graduate education and early career in Washington, DC, to the most important aspect of Minimalism—the loosening up of categories like painting and sculpture. This freedom allowed Gilliam to fit his work among the triad of methodology (his own), art historiography (that resisted placing him), and spatial depth (defined by flat painting versus sculpture in the round). It is tempting to call Gilliam's work Postminimalist, but I would resist the urge in favor of simply describing what *Autumn Surf* made visible: Gilliam was interested in the exploration of shapes within an extended topography. *Autumn Surf* spread up and out in the gallery, speaking to his interest in architecture, geometry, industry, landscape, organic forms, and the interaction of all with color. Color! Pure color—whether stained, soaked, sprayed, rubbed in, or piled on—drove the installation. *Autumn Surf* is a hinge in Gilliam's practice, showing how his work matured up to that moment and giving clues as to what was to come as he continued to evolve as an artist.

In 2018, while in Basel, Switzerland, for an extended period installing an exhibition,[3] Gilliam noticed that the city's population had grown more international with an influx of migrants from across the world. Watching the daily news there made him more attuned to the plight of dislocated peoples, specifically those from parts of Africa. This line of thought led him back to previous interests in the forms of "early Africa"—the triangulated pyramid and the flat-roofed *mastaba*—that had captivated him as a student. He describes the intensity of being aware of the "agony of people who are dislocated" alongside the knowledge of the rich legacy of their ancestral achievements.[4] His most recent sculptures, begun shortly after his return to his DC studio following the Basel exhibition opening, are centered around elemental forms (specifically, the pyramid and circle) and his earliest innovations in process: pouring raw paint onto canvas, allowing pigment to saturate, and stretching canvases over a beveled edge. The result is a body of work consisting of monochromatic pyramidal sculptures and concentric circle wall reliefs, along with new beveled-edge paintings on canvas and painted works on paper. Though distinct objects, they are interconnected (comprised of at least two series) and sensitively unified like an installation.

"...working with cubes and trying on shapes."

From his earliest work making depth in his painted canvases, stretching them across two bars, Gilliam has been in conversation with the sculptural, if not actual sculpture. He prefers to think of his work as an extension of not only his painting practice but also an understanding of the medium of painting.[5] Gilliam is not

fig. 2
Robert Ryman
Varese Wall, 1975
polyvinyl acetate emulsion on wood with steel bars and foam blocks
96 × 288 × 12"
Dia Art Foundation. Gift of The Greenwich Collection, Ltd.

unusual in his insistence on the medium of paint over the method of its delivery. Jo Baer and Robert Ryman have defined their works as painting, regardless of form or ground. Ryman even used the term "three-dimensional paintings" to describe a group of his free-standing and partially wall-mounted objects (fig. 2), which might otherwise have been called "sculpture." Similarly Anne Truitt (whom Gilliam knew well in DC) used the sculptural form to enhance the presence of her painterly surfaces, which often operated as variant grounds for her steady hand and tonal complexities.

The progression from the beveled canvases to draping cloth over existing elements to the addition of visible three-dimensional objects, like stones or lumber in his 1960s and 1970s installations, speaks to his desire to work *in space*. But this is born out of a greater connection to the architecture of a given space. This is certainly true of his pyramids, which grew out of seeing the small, leftover pieces of the basic cubic structures as they returned from the fabricators and finding the "irregularity of the block of wood…inspiring."[6] First he strung six wood polygon pieces along a metal bar. Then he suspended the bar in the middle of an open-faced case. The wood pieces (some white, others in rainbow colors) are stained so you can see the grain of the wood and feel the balance between the added color and the wood's natural tonalities. The moveable units resemble an abacus. Despite the name given to the series and the reference to the calculating tool, there is only one bar, so Gilliam's abacus cannot be used to count or measure. Instead the wooden digits slide over and across the single bar, referencing the larger pyramids that he worked on simultaneously.

The Pyramids are composite floor pieces erected in two sizes: a large one that rises to eight feet and several smaller ones that top out at five feet. Gilliam, inspired by the remote-control toy cars in his studio, placed wheels on them, lifting the structures slightly off the floor to give them the appearance of hovering. Constructed from wood, each piece is a single, solid color (some jewel tones and white) from top to bottom, which is sequentially broken up by a recurrent, lateral aluminum insertion—suggestive of the stepped construction of a monumental pyramid. Gilliam cites his attraction to making a pyramidion object as born from encountering ancient pyramids (like those in Egypt), calling forth our desire for more contact with something larger, rather than smaller, because "pyramids angle to a point. When you are standing it moves away from you."[7] His effort to replicate the corporeal experience of monumentality resembles his interest in installation, wherein "everyone is in the work."[8] To move around the structures is similar to interacting with *Autumn Surf*: you can come in, move out of or around it, but it must be confronted in some way.

The strong sense of play in Gilliam's tabletop abacus and moveable pyramids permeates much of his practice. In recalling the installation of *Autumn Surf*, he noted that children knew immediately how to experience it: they ran around it, tried to go under it, or found their way into the center of the drapes and folds; whereas adults initially stood cautiously at the edge of the work before venturing closer. The element of play is crucial here, not simply because he wants us—the viewers of his installations—to immerse ourselves in his work but also because play is key to fully embodying something. Play requires both comfort and flexibility, being able to go with the flow of a concept, no matter where it takes you. This is true in both a mental and physical sense.

It is no surprise then that Gilliam cites Christo and Jeanne-Claude, Ornette Coleman, Philip Glass, Yvonne Rainer, and David Smith as important interlocutors for his formal and conceptual way of working in space. Each engages a form of play.[9] Poignantly he speaks of Rainer as "not the kind of artist that is always an artist."[10] This description could easily apply to how he wills the viewer to come and engage (in other words, *to play*) with his three-dimensional works, while always maintaining that they are part of a painting practice. When I asked Gilliam what these works (both his older installations and his more recent objects) were if not sculpture, he replied that he had been simply "working with cubes and trying on shapes"[11]—a statement that playfully obscures his studied, careful approach to working on ideas over time to allow for refinement. As an artist, he acts as an agent activating the artwork, which is a way of side-stepping the limited definition of an artist as only a maker of objects. Notably each of these artists' practices activates variation from a known form—be it dance for Rainer, classical music for Glass and Coleman (particularly true of Coleman's further departure from jazz into free jazz), and sculpture for Christo and Jeanne-Claude.

While preparing to install his exhibition at Dia: Beacon in 2019, he shipped a single blue hoop along with the other elements that would comprise the suspended draped painting, which was the show's central focus. The circular hoop is the basic form from which the Circles are derived. Like the Abacuses and Pyramids, the Circles are constructed of pigment-dyed wood. Each is a wall-mounted relief composed of interconnecting concentric circles that radiate out from a central negative space. Made in separate pieces, once connected, the seams between the parts are visible. The void in the center is surrounded by a recessed, brushed aluminum circle that draws light to the construction. Gilliam connects this body of work to Kenneth Noland's seminal Concentric Circle series (1958–63, fig. 3)—more commonly known as his "target" paintings because rings of color surround a central, circular point in each of the canvases. Noland frequently alternated light and dark colors in varying widths or allowed bands of unprimed canvas to peek through his compositions to magnify their surface light. Gilliam achieves something similar with the aluminum and visible seams, where the parts of the circles connect to each other to emanate light and suggest total depth.

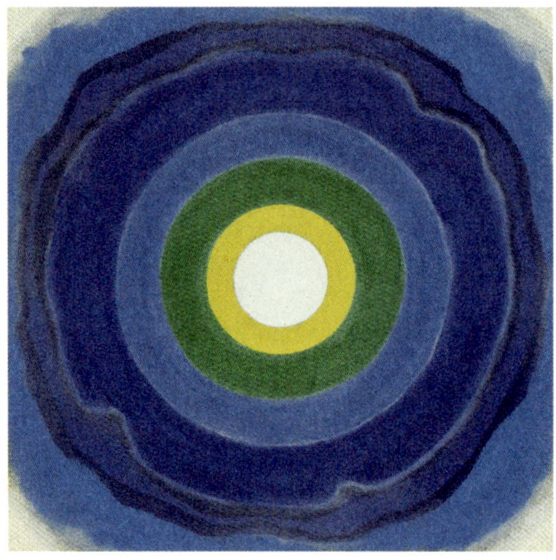

fig. 3
Kenneth Noland
April, 1960
acrylic on canvas
16 × 16"
The Phillips Collection, Washington, DC. Acquired 1960

In later conversations he revealed that the hoop was his referent for play as a fundamental aspect of his practice, one that he traced back to his study of paintings, like Pieter Bruegel the Elder's *Kinderspiele* (*Children's Games*) (1560, fig. 4) in which a male and female figure use sticks to roll hoops (hers adorned with bells, no less) in the foreground. This painting's focus on children at play has long been understood as an explication of humanism, with the child functioning as a visual metaphor for the inherent goodness of human beings.[12] Gilliam's take on play has a similar aim for both the art object and the viewer. He sets up both as

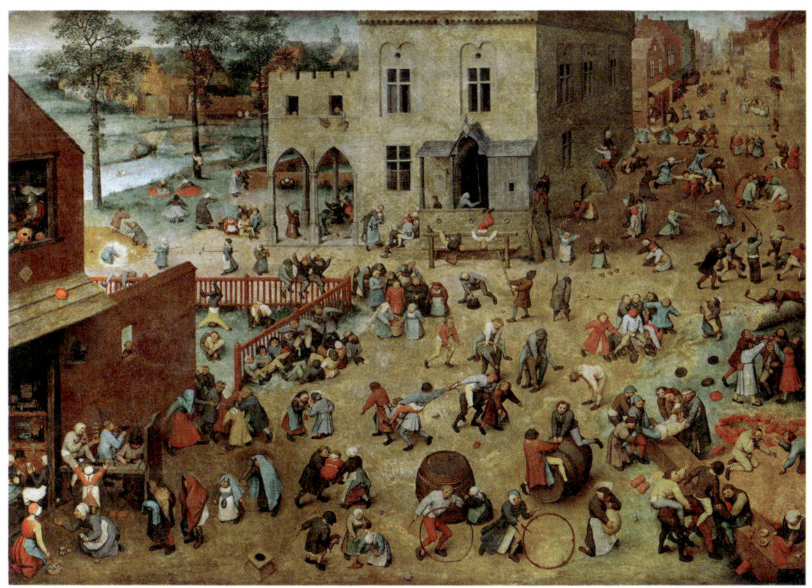

fig. 4
Pieter Bruegel the Elder
Kinderspiele (*Children's Games*), 1560
oil on wood
46 7/16 × 63 3/8"
Kunsthistorisches Museum, Vienna

equally eligible for activation and variation through the interplay of one to the other. If humanism stresses a kind of commonality of the human experience and, thus, the ability to use ration as a method of problem-solving, then the viewer of his art can figure out what to do once in the presence of art. Hence the unfettered reaction of the children who saw *Autumn Surf* versus that of the adults, who needed more time to react and act on their instincts.

Placeholders

Gilliam describes his recent works on paper as placeholders, a term that defines the way that they are hung as visual directives, "positioned on the wall to be seen in regards to the rest of the show."[13] The rest of the show—the free-standing Pyramids and the Circle reliefs—forms a unified installation, though each object is an individual work of art. Gilliam's holistic approach to this new body of work derives from his earlier room-scaled installations that he ceased producing in 1980. Starting in the late 1970s Gilliam began experimenting with paper before settling on washi, the traditional Japanese paper, which is handmade from the inner bark of specific trees and plants—primarily Gampi and Mitsumata shrubs and Mulberry (Kozo) bush. The bark's fibrous nature creates a paper that can take on applied color well and be handled more easily than other paper types. In a prolonged manner, Gilliam first wets down the paper with pigment paint (by spraying it or working it with a rag) to such a degree that he nearly saturates it back to pulp. This achieves what he calls "solid color"—the paper's complete and total saturation with

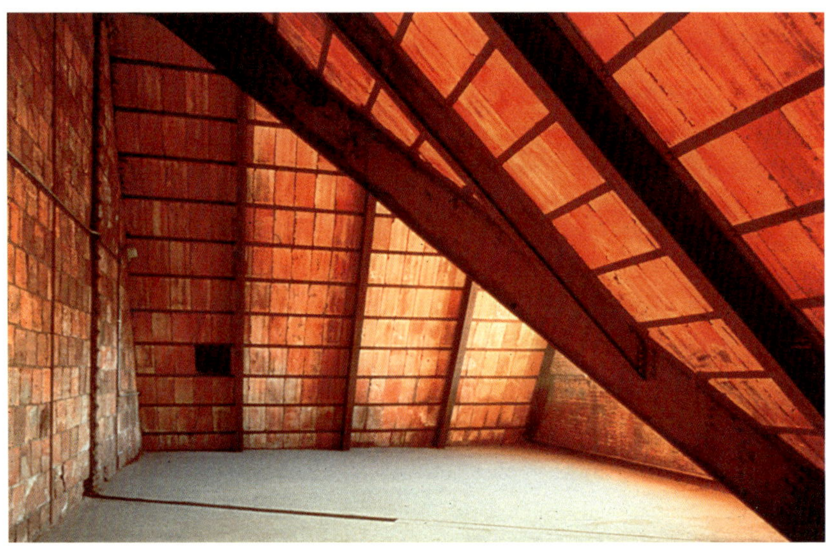

fig. 5

Richard Serra
Untitled, 1976

Installation view of *Rooms*, P.S.1, Long Island City, New York, June 9–June 26, 1976

the intended color. Over time he has learned the balance of working with paper and found his own peace with it: "It is nothing more than a print...it is fragile."[14] Working with the paper is a slow process. The color has to be built up gradually so that the paper does not tear, and each layer of paint dries and hardens to allow for the next. This process is an adaptation of the technique he has used on canvas (whether natural or synthetic) for nearly sixty years.

The square or rectangular sheets (some deep and dark, like the black and blue-hued Ad Reinhardt paintings that he has so admired over the years, while others are lighter in tone) are nearly indistinguishable from recto to verso. Each sheet is a solid color field that may stand alone as a tone or be matched in variance to form a color sequence. Hung on the wall, they are literally color holding a place, demarcating a distinct space through what appears to be color only, since the saturation of pigment nearly removes the paper's physical presence. Gilliam's concept of placeholding references the "old term for teaching math"[15] that allows for something to denote a missing quantity by effectively filling in for it. In relation to the other two- and three-dimensional elements, the works on paper represent and reflect their pigments and maintain the centrality of color to the conception of his process. They also point back to the entire body of paintings that preceded them—he sees them as having "isolated color" out of his multihued paintings, like *Autumn Surf*, which was soaked and stained in multiple paint colors.[16] Each work on paper is an index to the individual colors that made up the earlier multi-colored compositions, allowing viewers to recall or identify colors present in other paintings.

When I asked Gilliam how his new artwork related to his previous work, he said that it did not.[17] Full stop. We then began a conversation about the installations that he had previously completed, before settling into a long discussion of *Autumn Surf*. *Works in Spaces* was, for Gilliam, what P.S.1's seminal, inaugural show of installation art, *Rooms* (fig. 5), was for Richard Serra three years later—an exhibition that allowed him to use the building as material that would be both an apex in his practice and a codex to his thought processes.[18] Gilliam was at the right stage personally (he turned forty in the fall of 1973) and professionally (he had been selected for the American pavilion in Venice the year before and had a solo museum exhibition) when he completed *Autumn Surf*. For an artist, creating an installation forces you to make a few or many things work together, whereas seeing an installation should reveal neither: few nor many. The inherent effort required should be visibly and, more importantly, experientially cohesive. And Gilliam's were just that—full, uninterrupted experiences. There is a seamless quality to the way in which the artist's latest works reference his known milestones—the tautly pulled bevels, the organic forms, the process-driven applications of paint—while also adding new, unexpected diversions into free-standing objects and materials used in totally different ways. These works come together as a cosmology, oscillating back and forth between what preceded them and what is yet to come. Gilliam is in a sweet spot once again.

1. Curated by Suzanne Foley, *Works in Spaces* was on view at the San Francisco Museum of Art from February 9 through April 8, 1973. For a longer discussion of the exhibition relative to Gilliam's practice, see Jonathan P. Binstock, *Sam Gilliam: A Retrospective* (Berkeley: University of California Press, 2005), 89–92, which remains the definitive exploration of the artist's work. I am thankful to Gilliam, Rockburne, and Naomi Spector Antonakos for their assistance in gathering information on and discussing *Works in Spaces* with me.

2. Sam Gilliam in conversation with the author, July 16, 2020.

3. Gilliam's first European retrospective, *The Music of Color: Sam Gilliam 1967–1973*, was on view at the Kunstmuseum Basel from June 9 through September 30, 2018. The exhibition was curated by Jonathan P. Binstock and the museum's director, Josef Helfenstein.

4. Sam Gilliam in conversation with the author, July 2, 2020.

5. See "Painting Objects: Robert Ryman's Three-Dimensional Paintings," in *Robert Ryman*, eds. Stephen Hoban and Courtney J. Martin (New Haven: Yale University Press and Dia Art Foundation, 2017), 277–93.

6. Sam Gilliam in conversation with the author, May 28, 2020.

7. Sam Gilliam in conversation with the author, July 2, 2020.

8. Ibid.

9. He cites Christo and Jeanne-Claude's Miami project, *Surrounded Islands* (1983), and the more recent opera by *Philip Glass, Appomattox* (2007/2015), as specific moments of aesthetic fascination and connection to his practice.

10. Sam Gilliam in conversation with the author, July 16, 2020.

11. Sam Gilliam in conversation with the author, August 8, 2020.

12. For a longer discussion of humanism and Brueghel's *Kinderspiele*, see Amy Orrock, "Homo ludens: Pieter Bruegel's Children's Games and the Humanist Educators," *Journal of Historians of Netherlandish Art* 4, no. 2 (Summer 2012), DOI: 10.5092/jhna.2012.4.2.1.

13. Sam Gilliam in conversation with the author, July 9, 2020.

14. Ibid.

15. Ibid.

16. Ibid.

17. Sam Gilliam in conversation with the author, May 26, 2020.

18. P.S.1's (now MoMA P.S.1) first exhibition, *Rooms*, was curated by founding director, Alanna Heiss. On view from June 9–26, 1976, it showcased installation art by seventy-eight artists throughout the interior and exterior of the building, a former elementary school. Given his prominence as an installation artist at this moment, Gilliam's absence from the show is notable. Antonakos and Bladen were, however, included in both the SFMoMA and P.S.1 exhibitions.

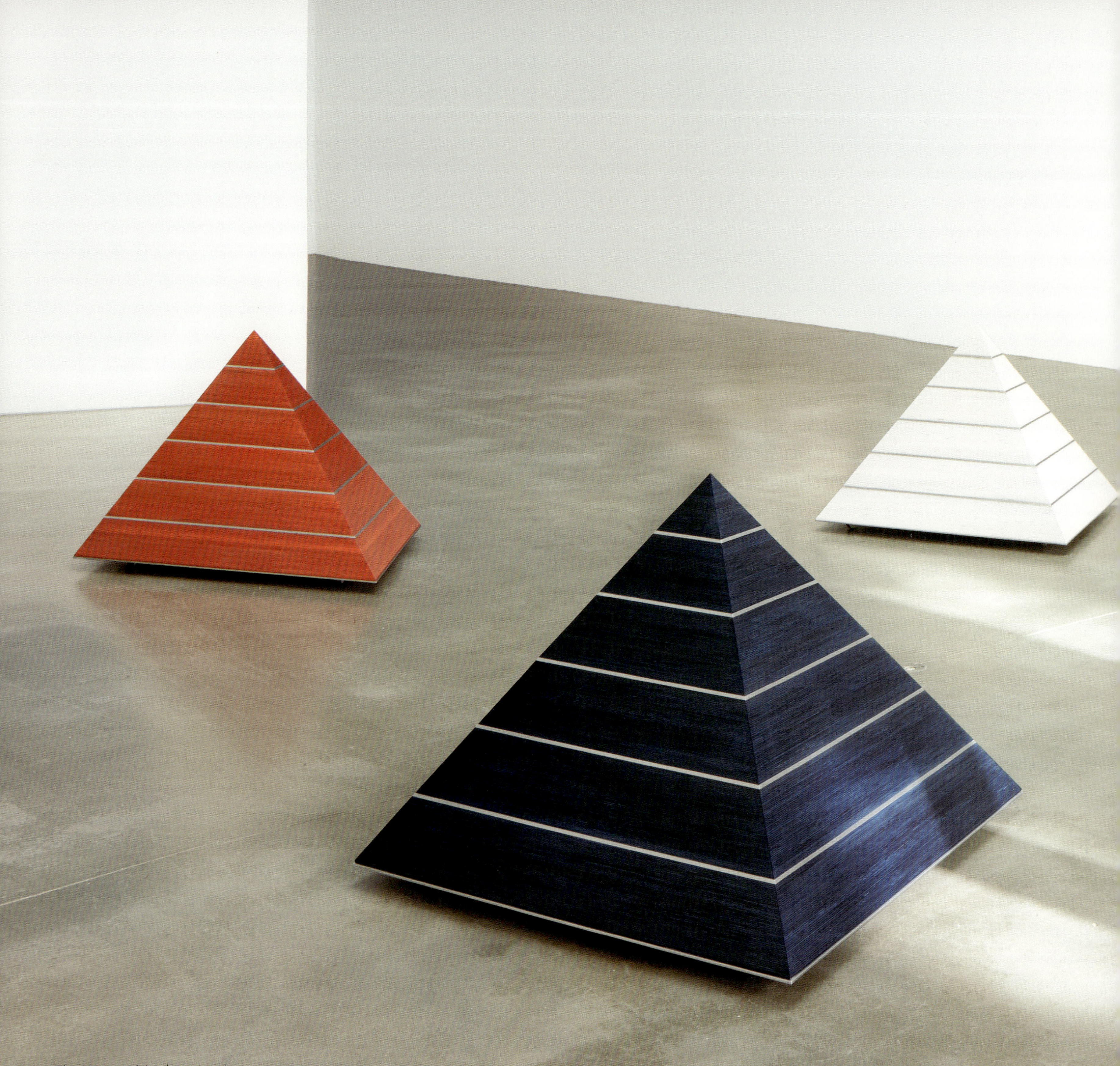

Five Pyramids | 2020 | wood, aluminum, die-stain, lacquer, 36 ¼ × 48 × 48" each, 5 total, overall dimensions variable

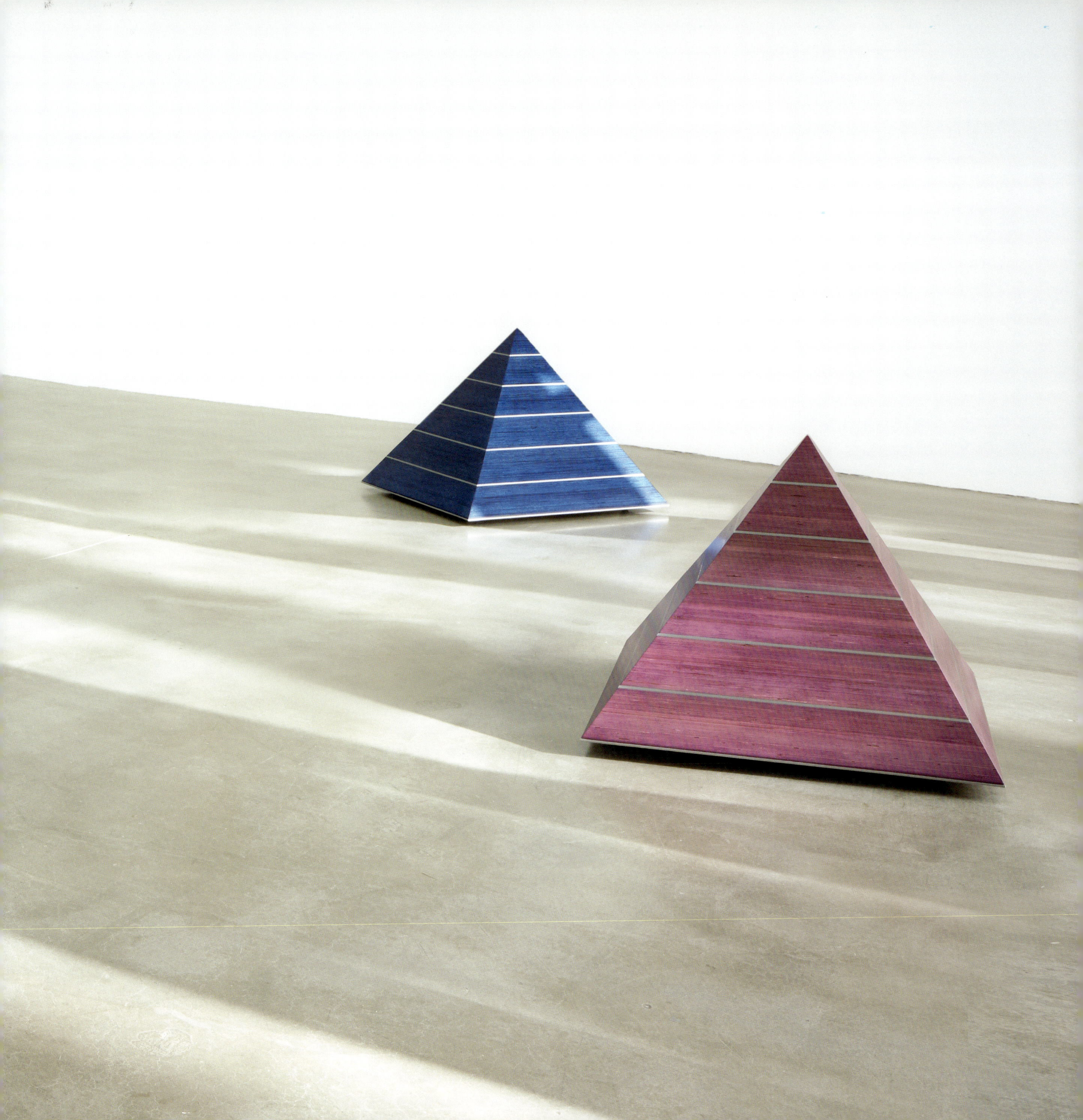

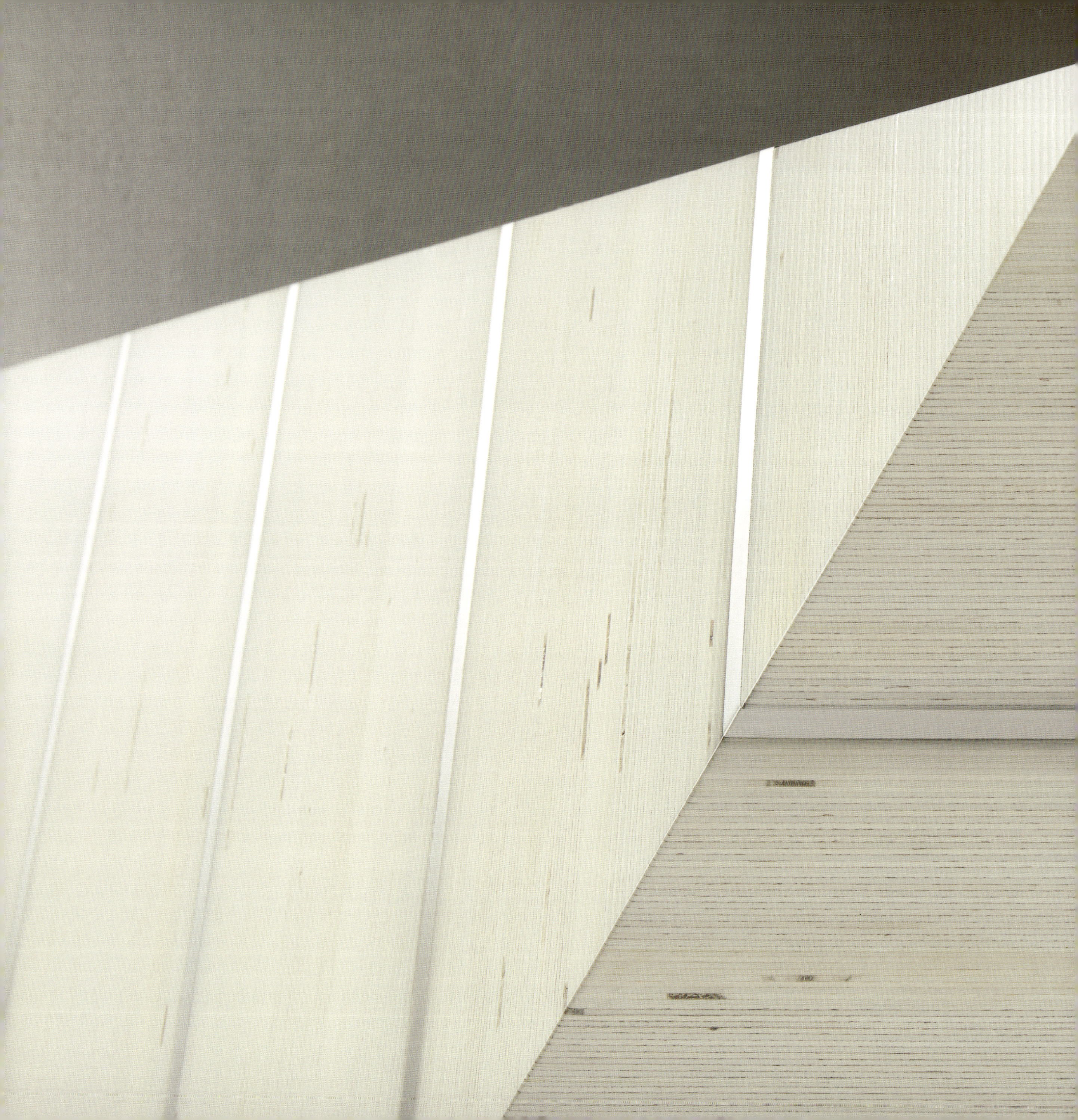

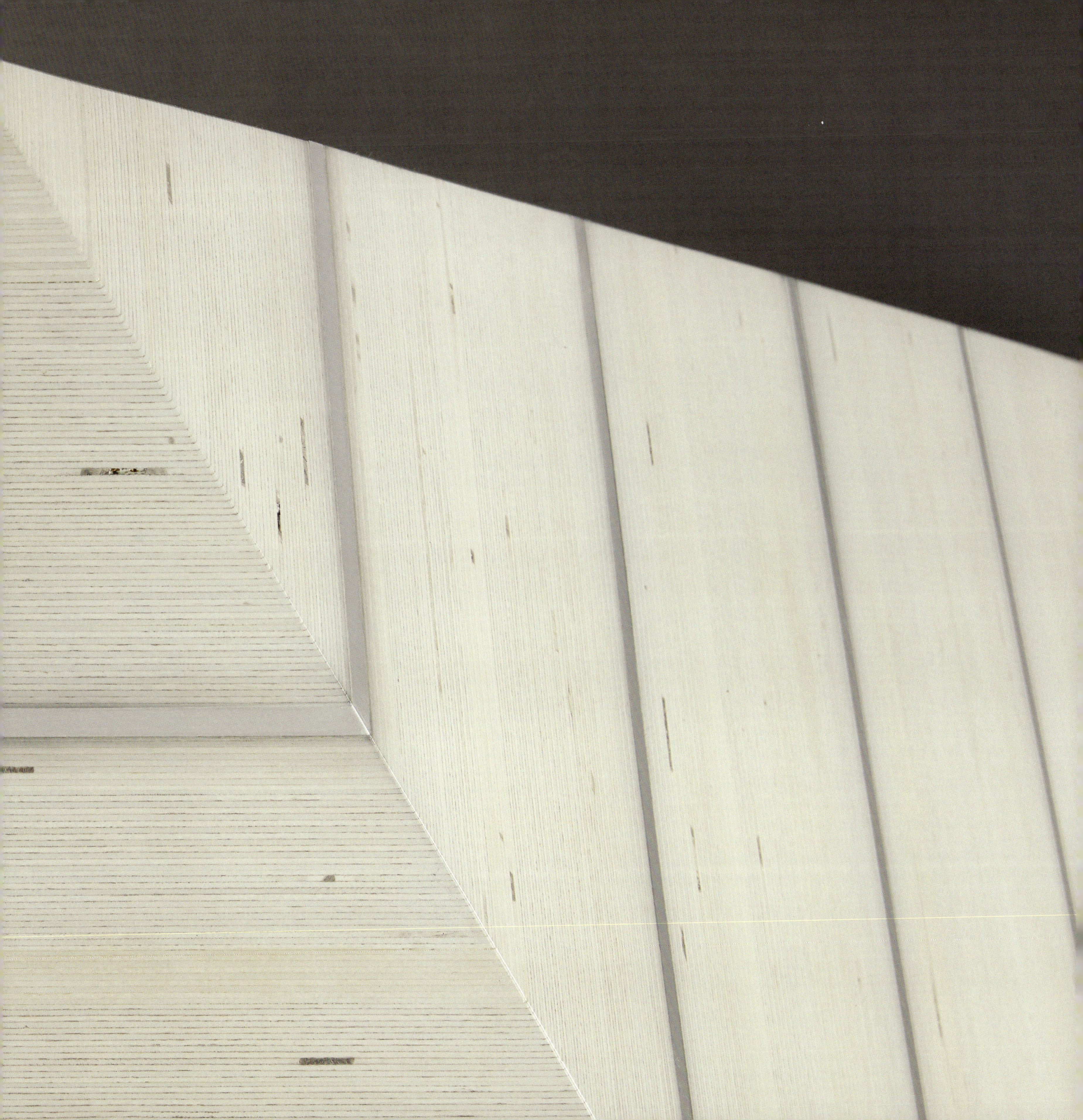

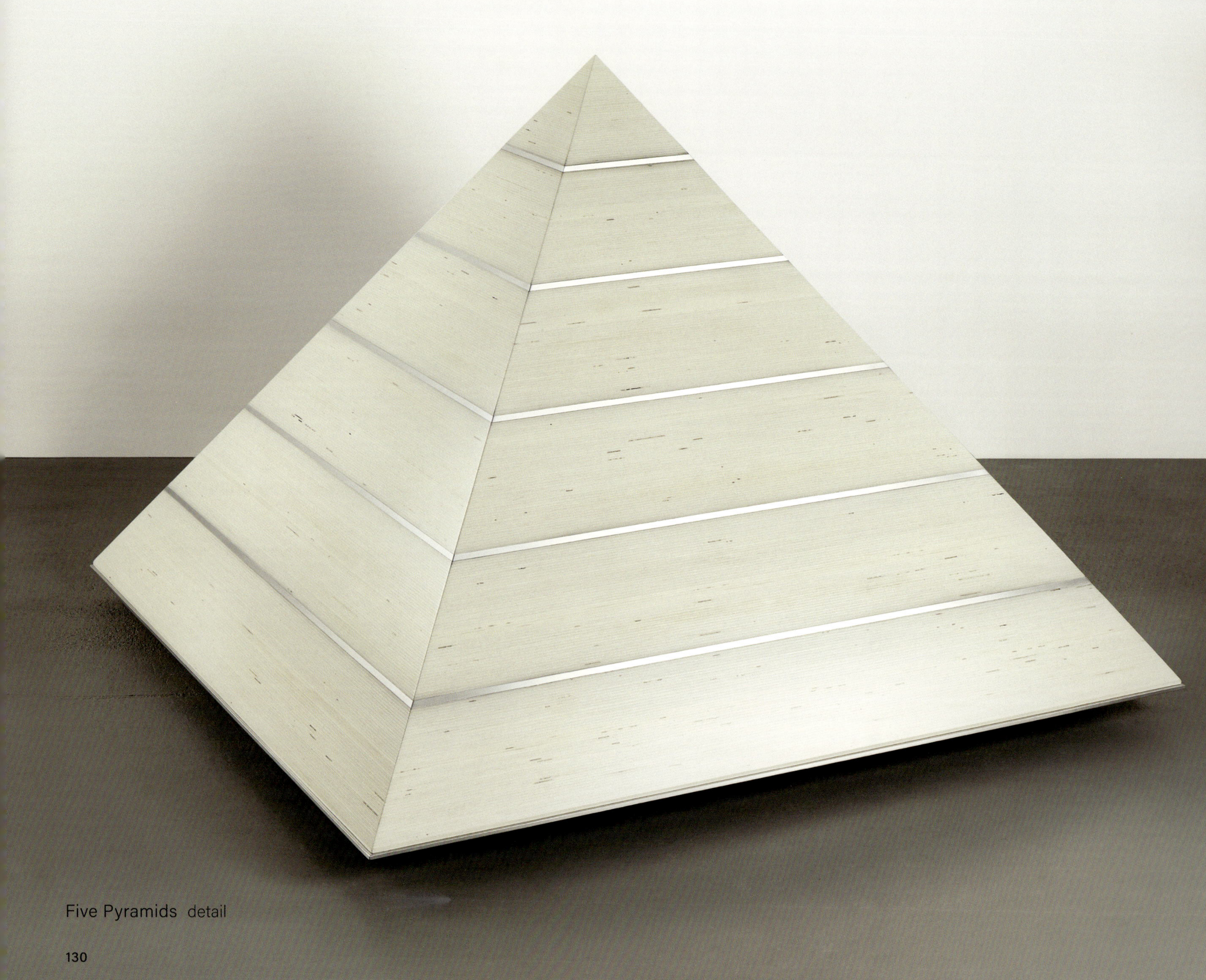

Five Pyramids detail

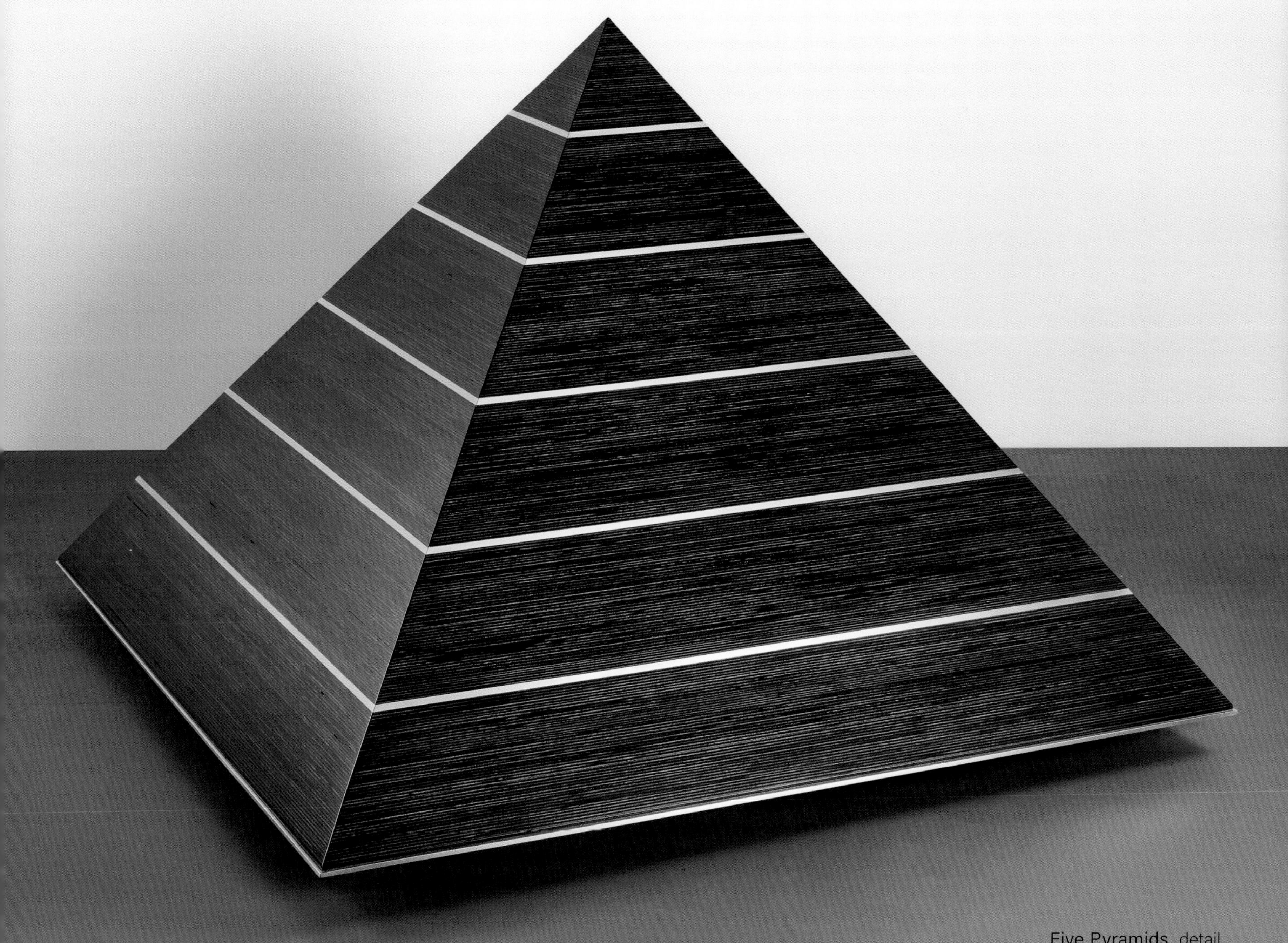

Five Pyramids detail

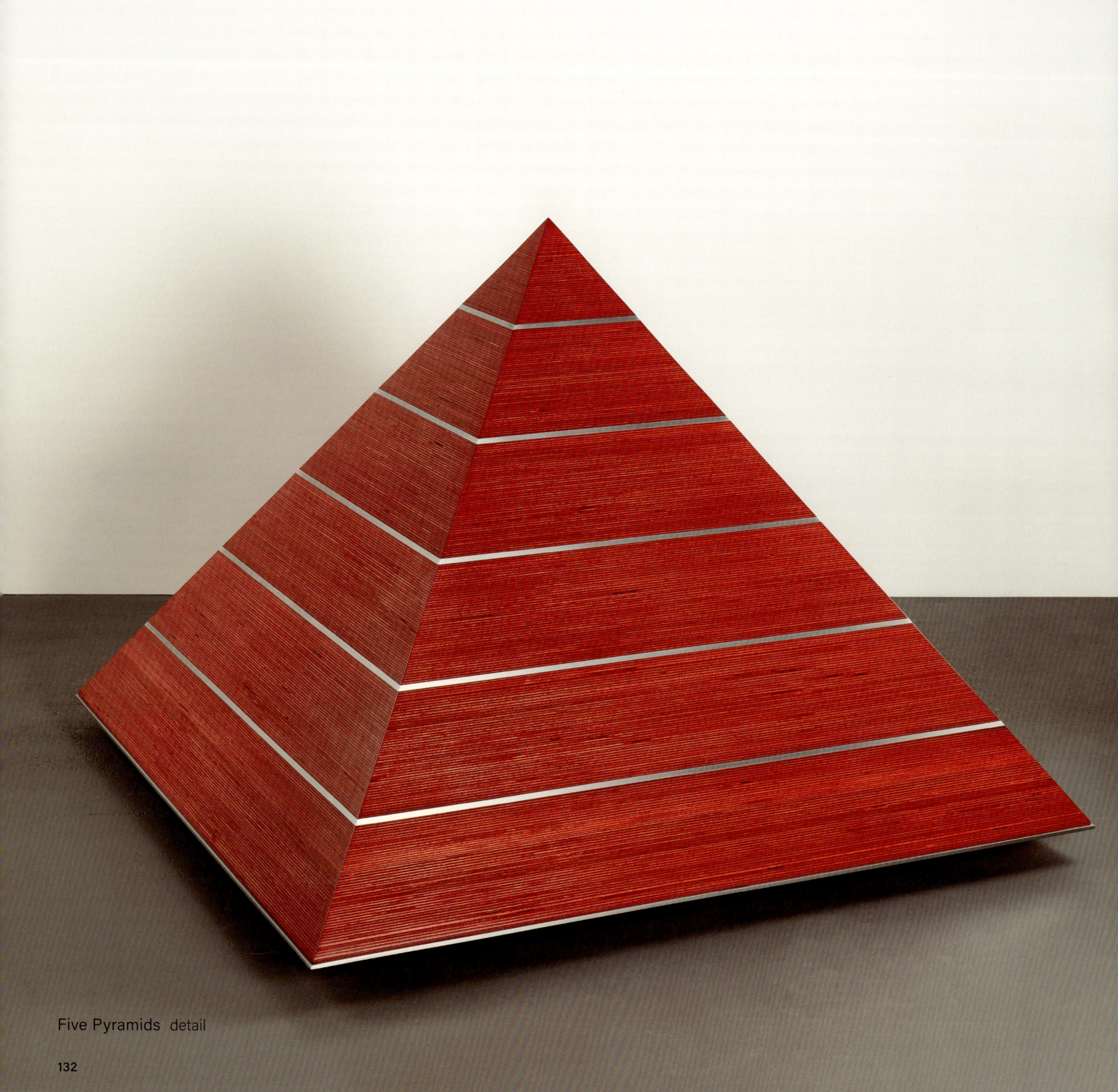

Five Pyramids detail

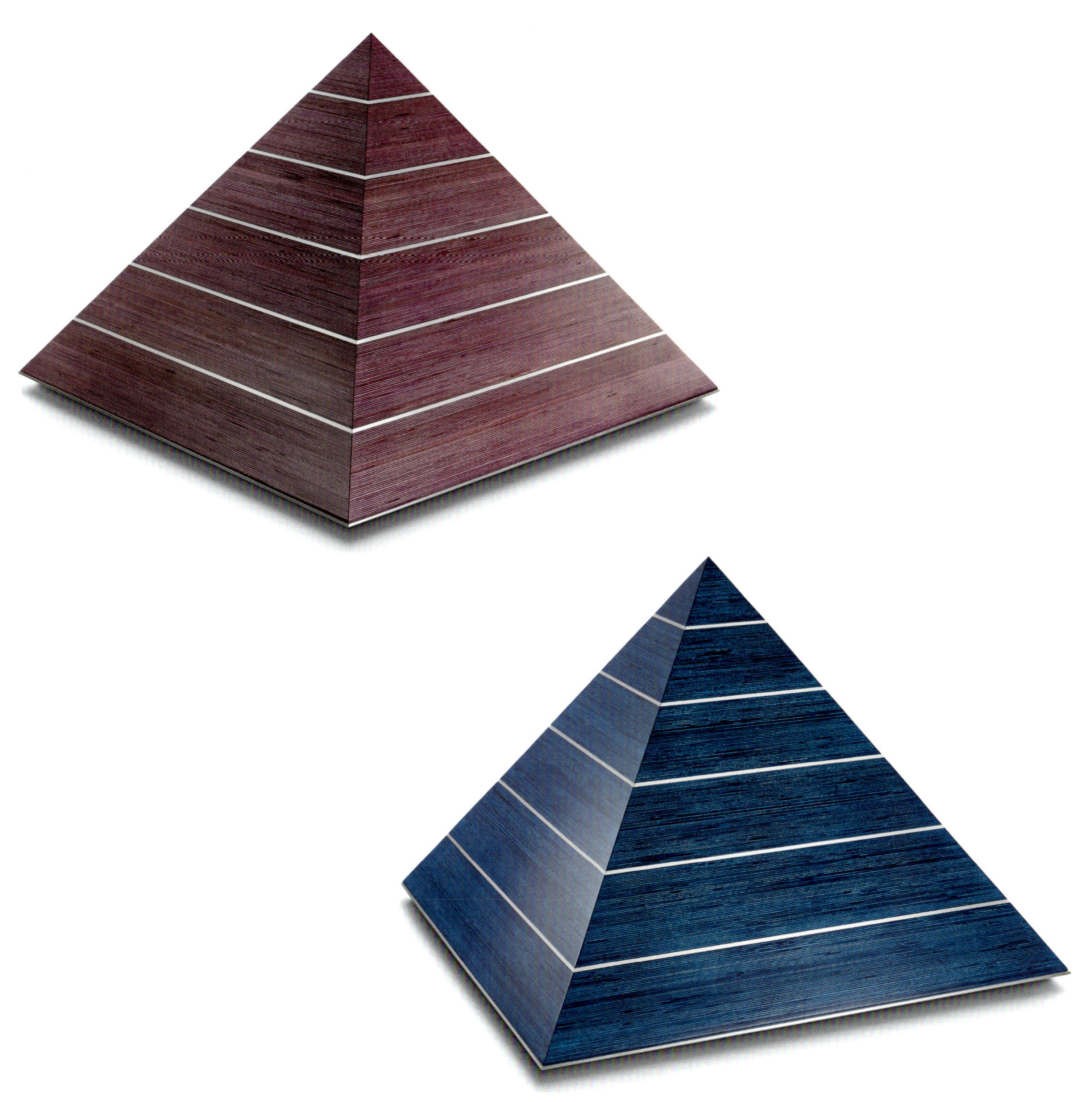

Five Pyramids details

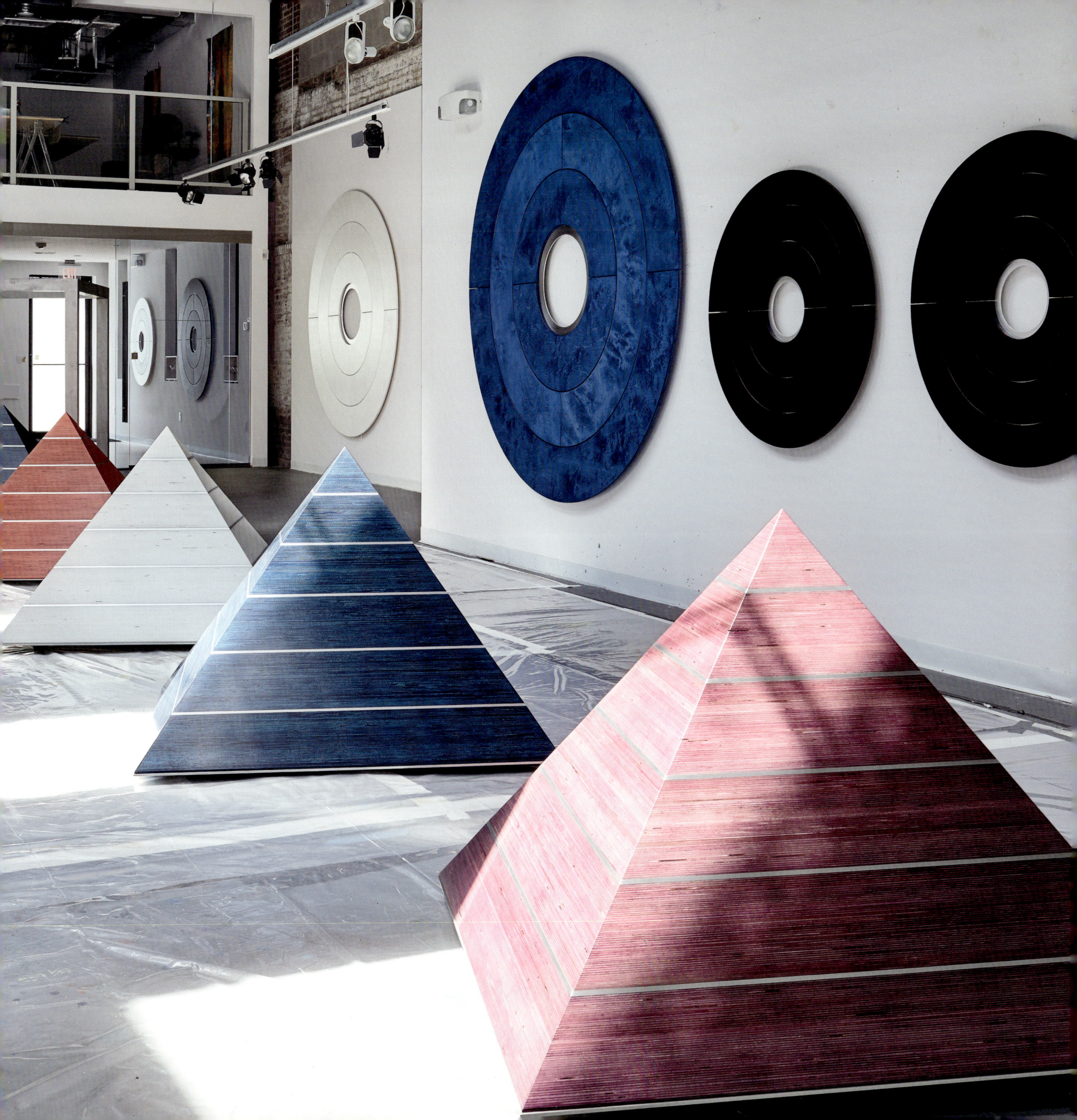

Three White Pyramids | 2020 | wood, aluminum, die-stain, lacquer, 36 ¼ × 48 × 48" each, 3 total, overall dimensions variable | variants 2, 3, and 4 of 5

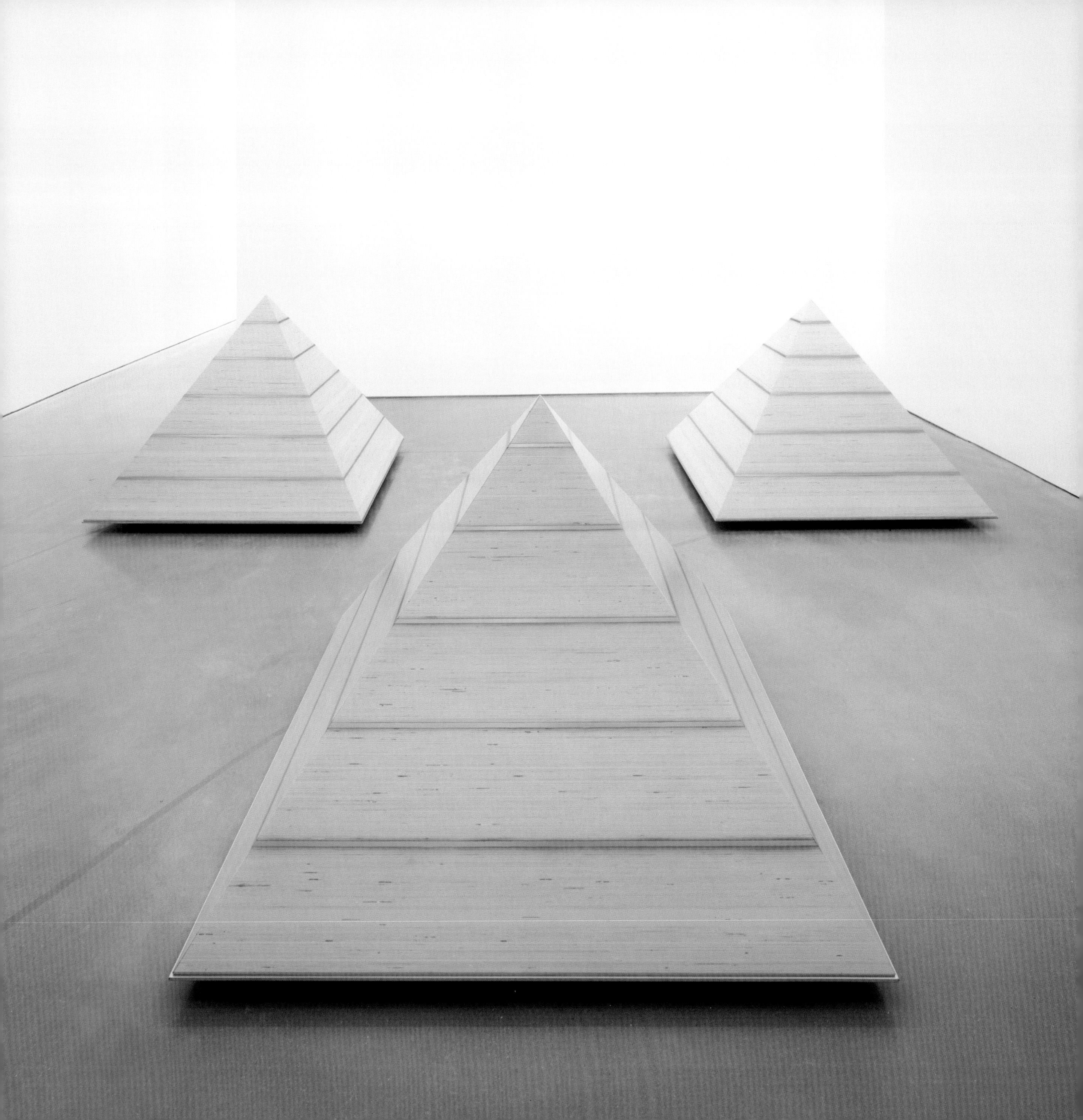

Pyramid | 2020 | wood, aluminum, die-stain, lacquer, 110 × 122 × 122"

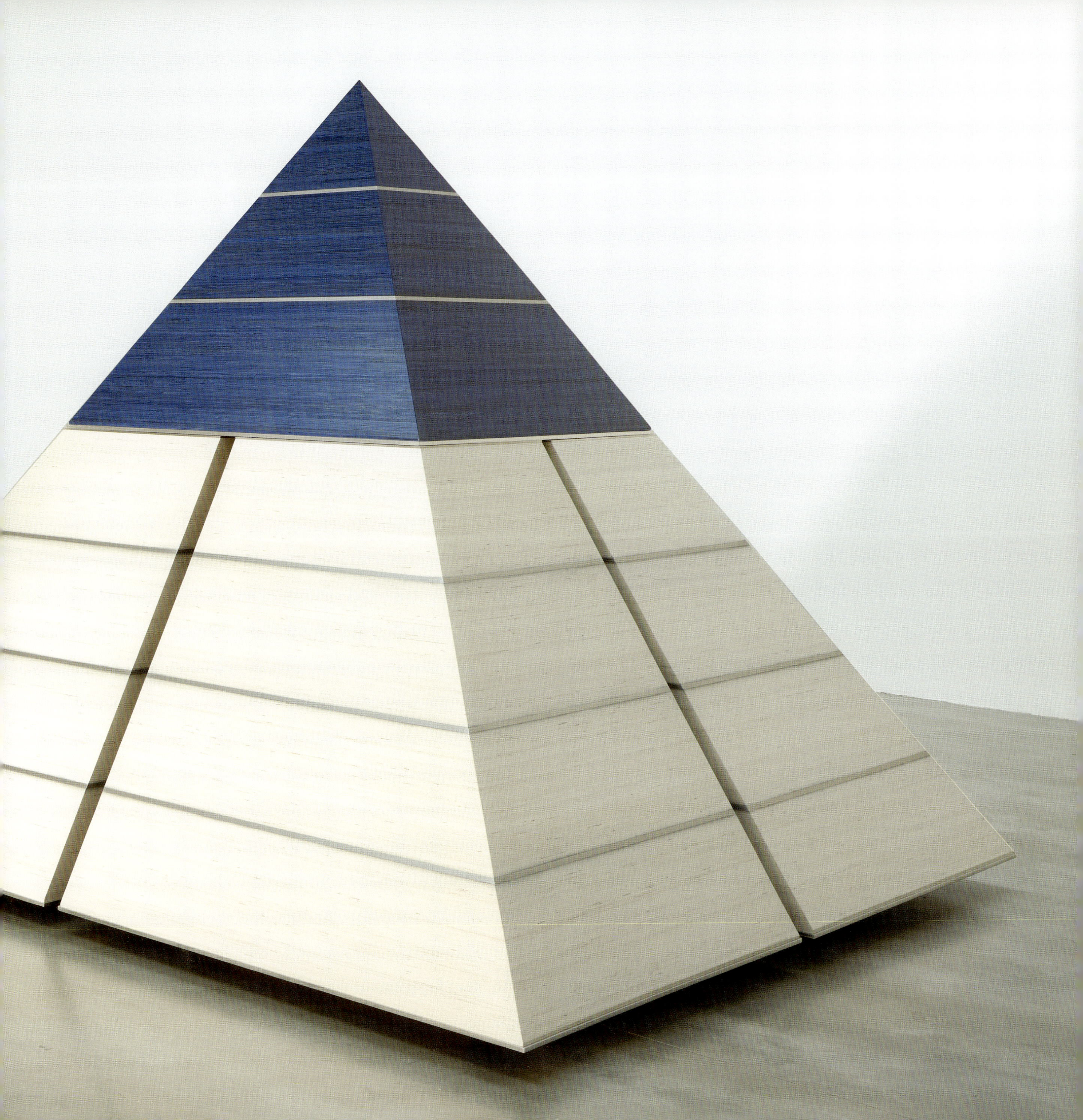

Mastaba (In Two Parts) | 2020 | wood, aluminum, die-stain, lacquer, 54 × 114 × 61"

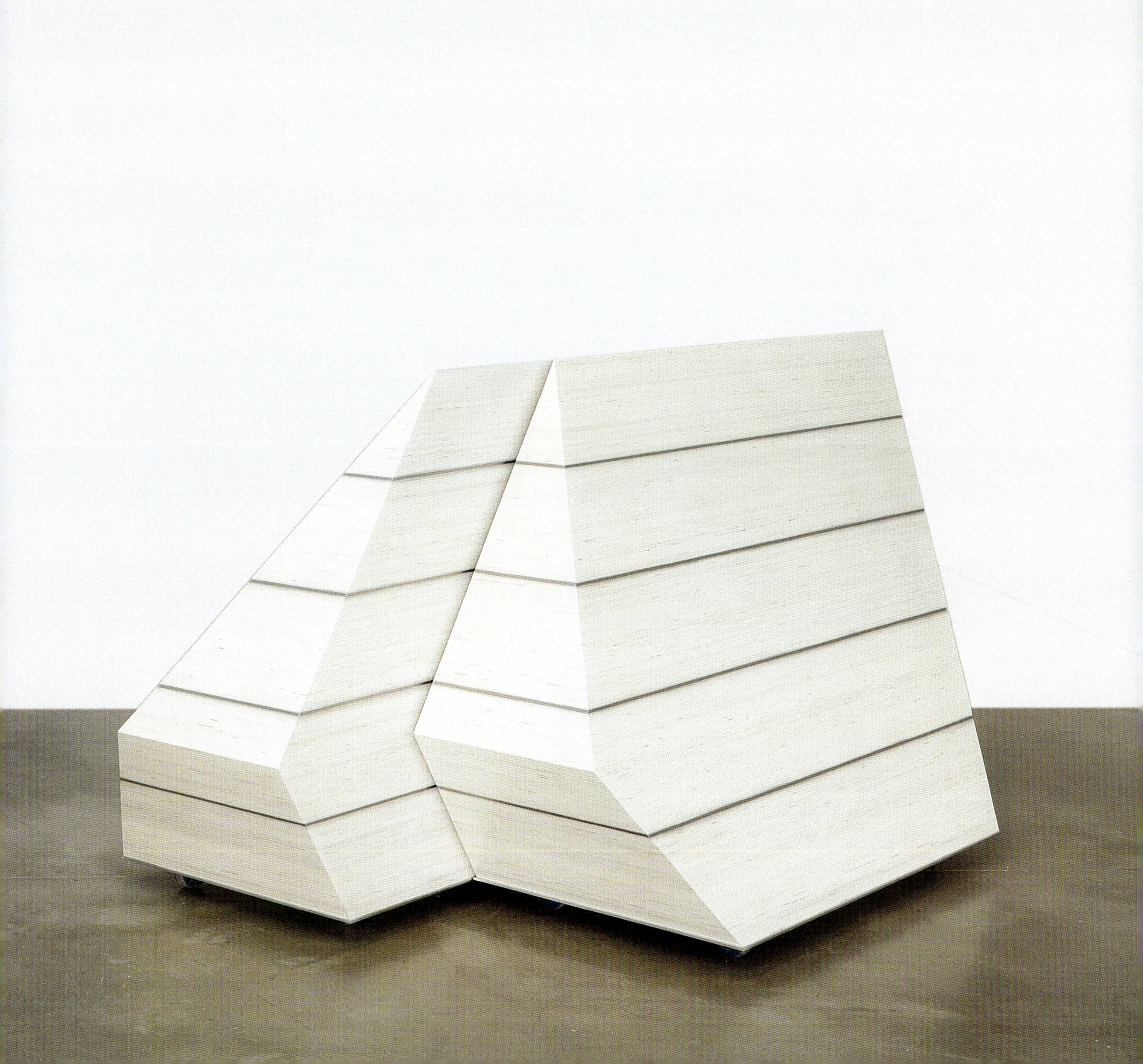

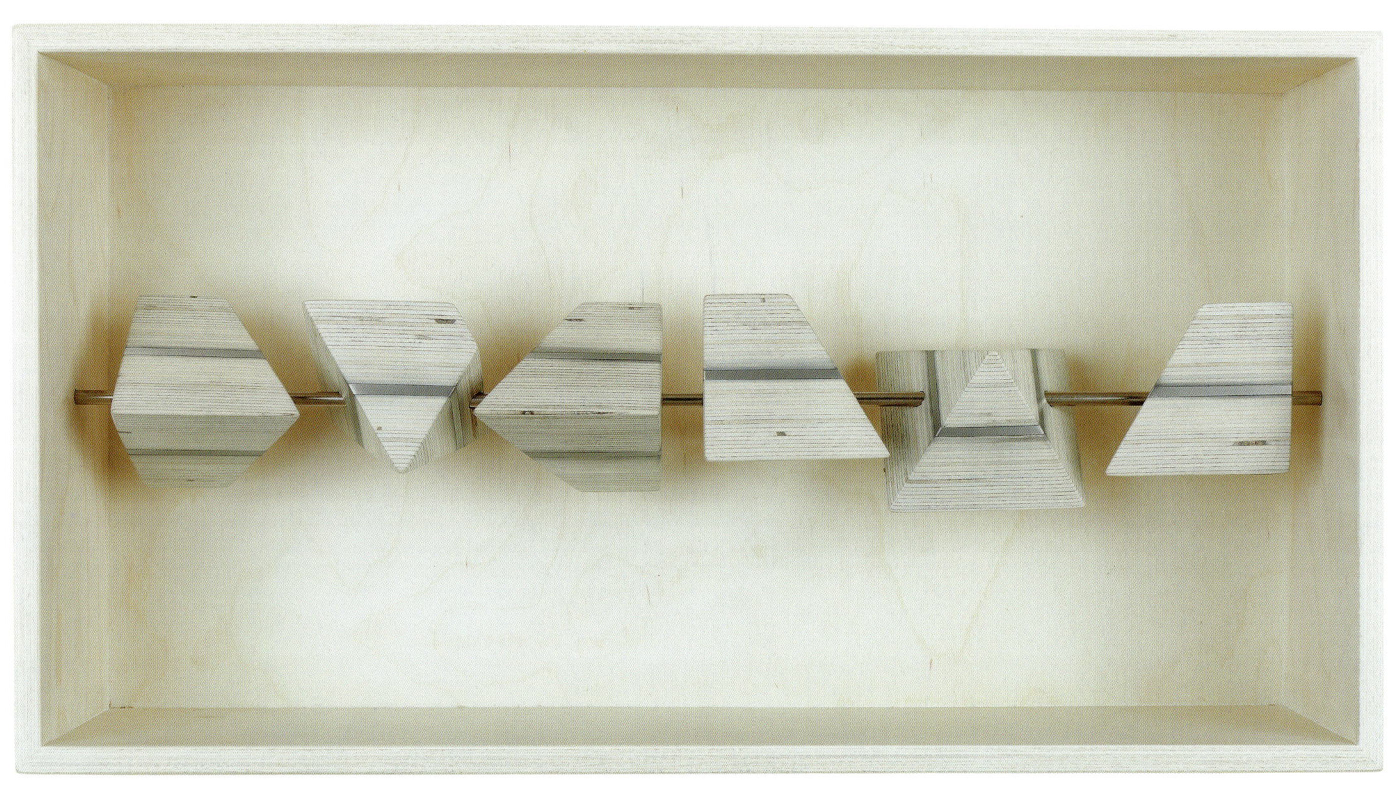

White Abacus | 2020 | wood, aluminum, die-stain, lacquer, 12 × 22 × 5" | variant 1 of 4

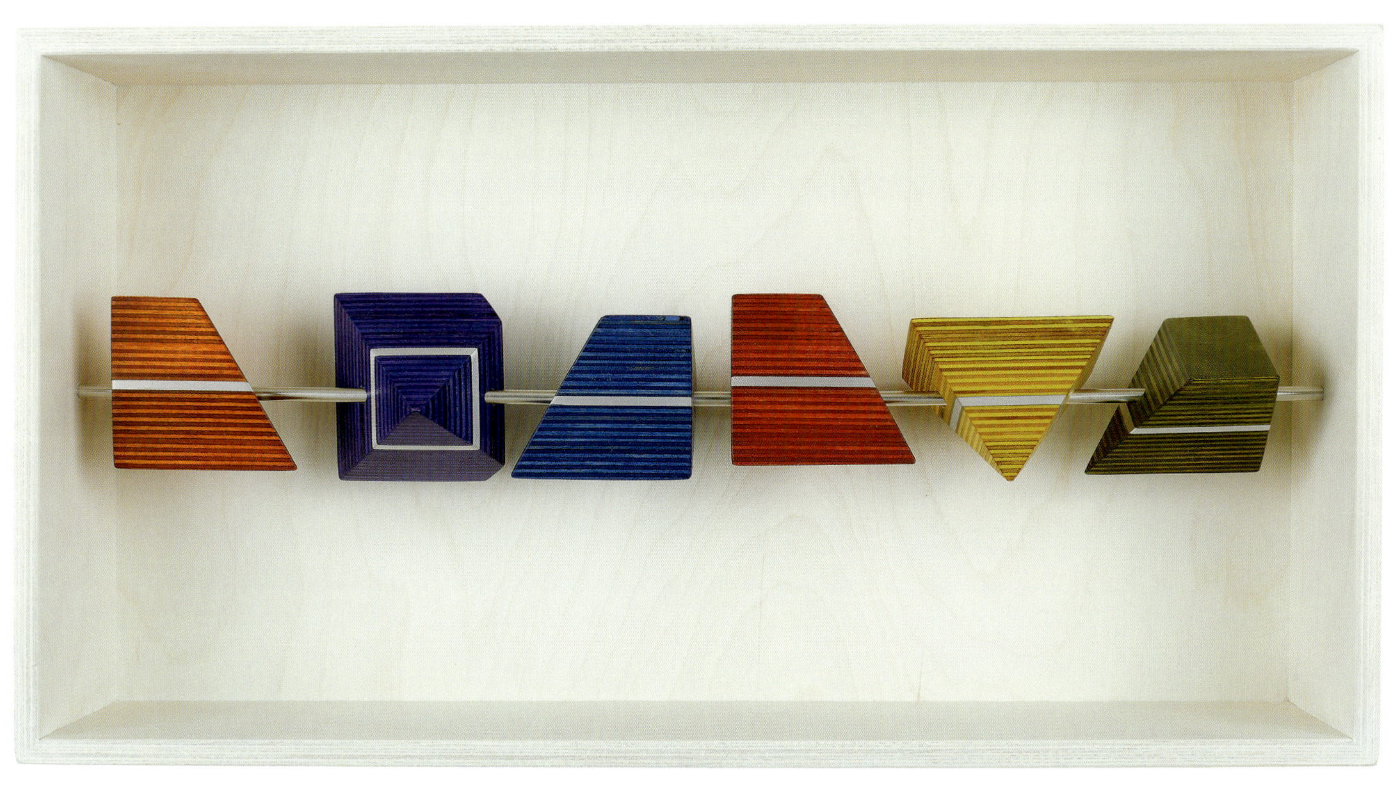

Color Abacus | 2020 | wood, aluminum, die-stain, lacquer, 12 × 22 × 5" | variant 1 of 4

This exhibition is dedicated to Barbara Rose

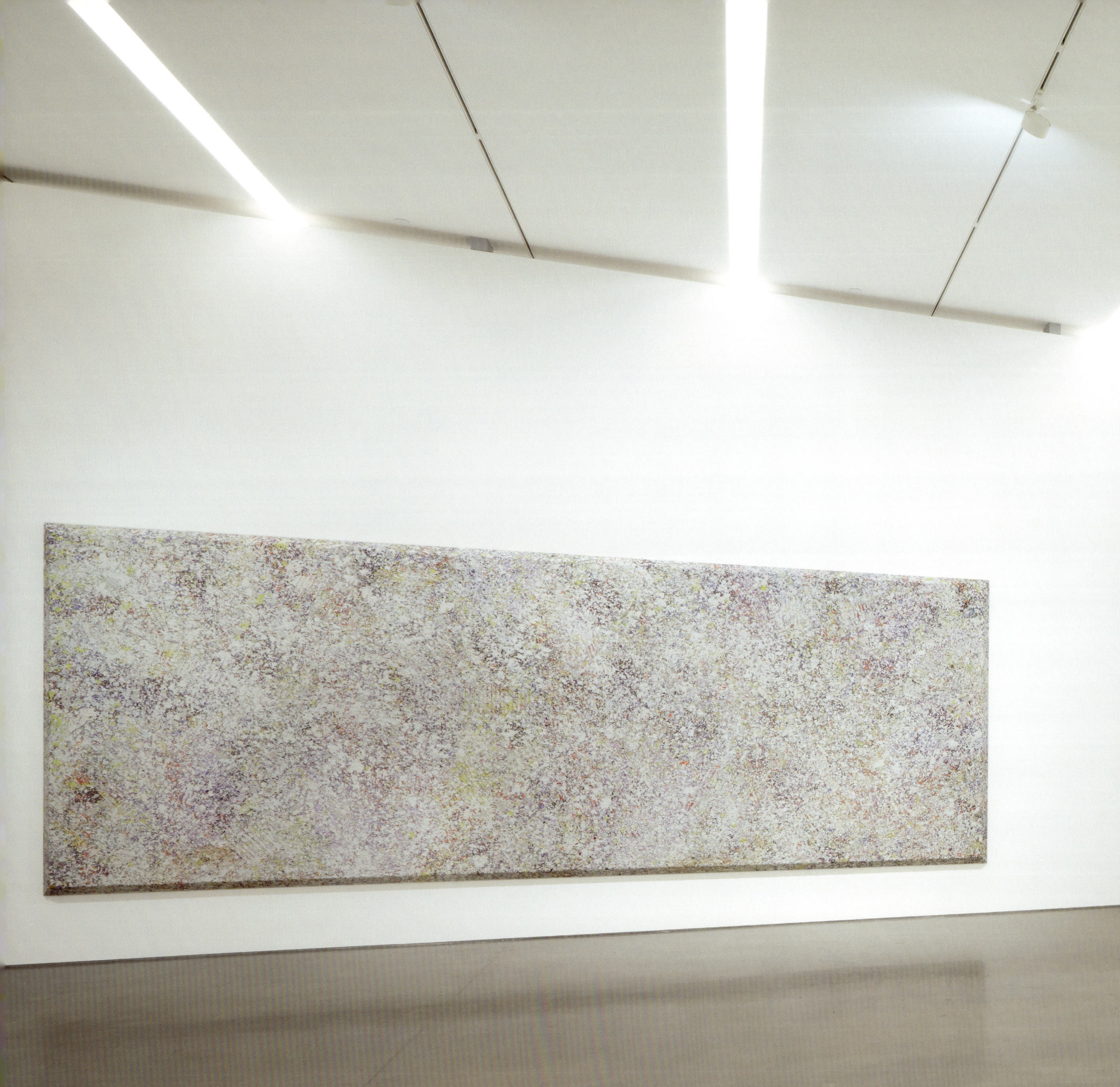

Installation view
540 West 25th Street

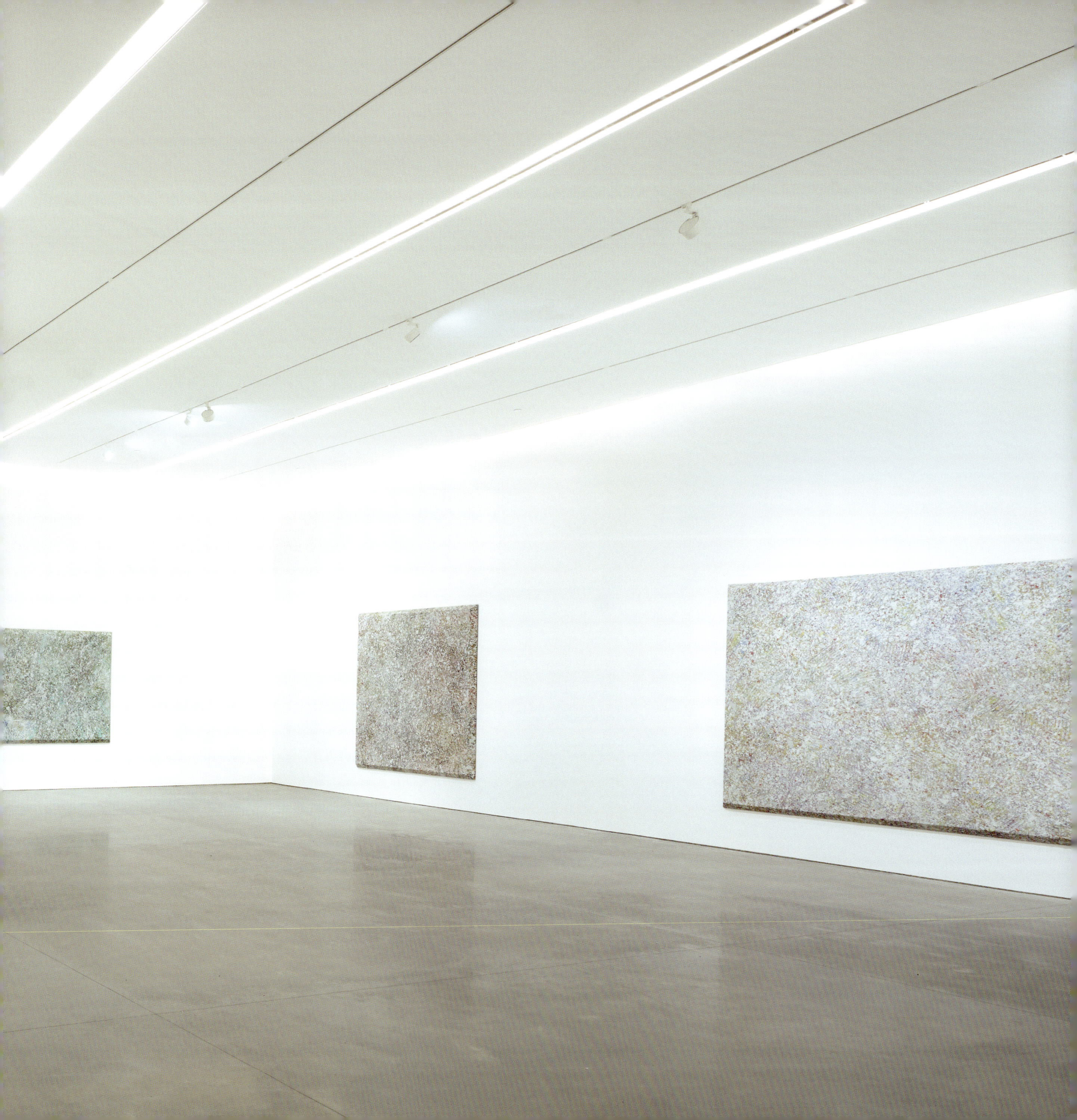

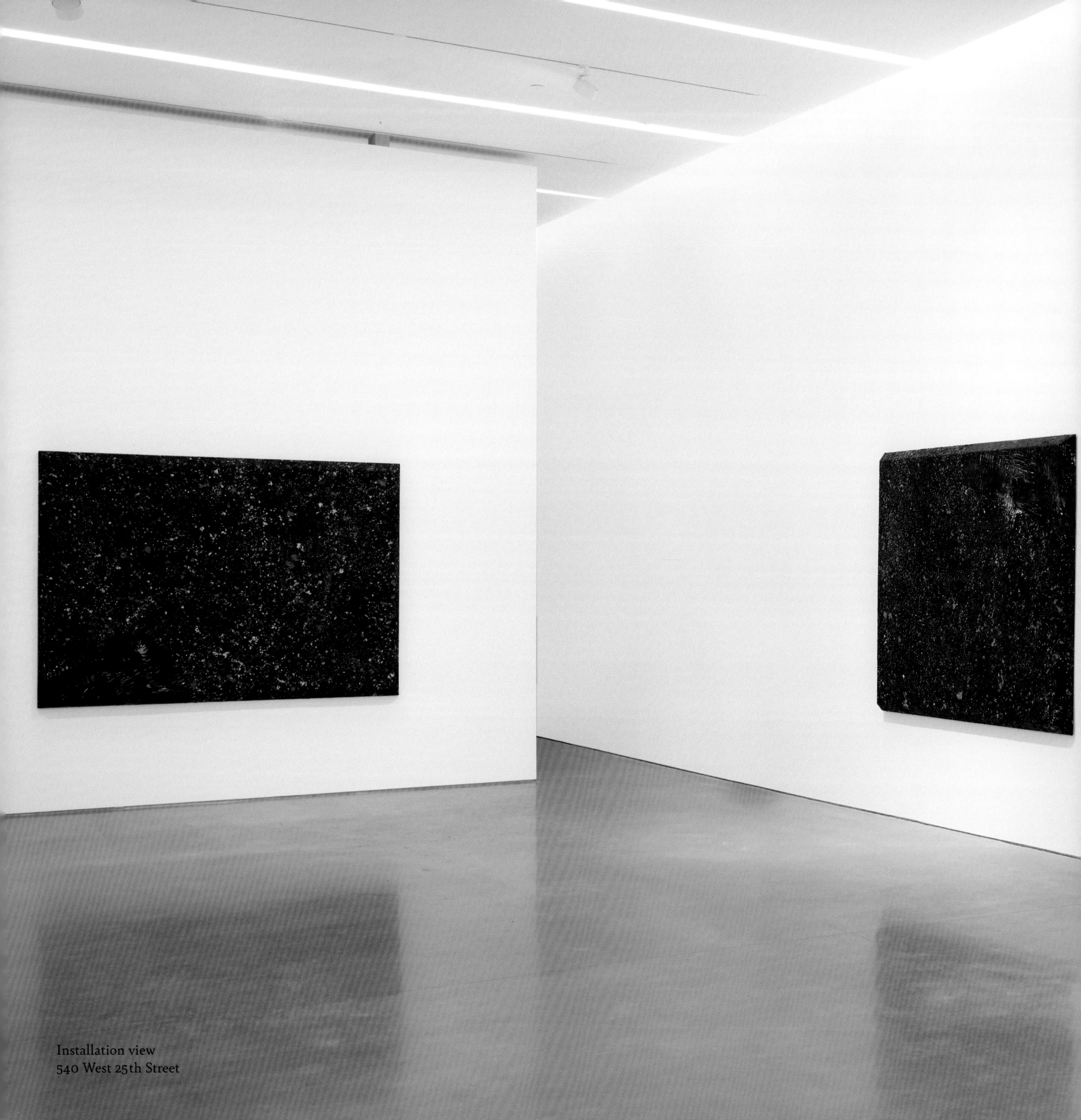

Installation view
540 West 25th Street

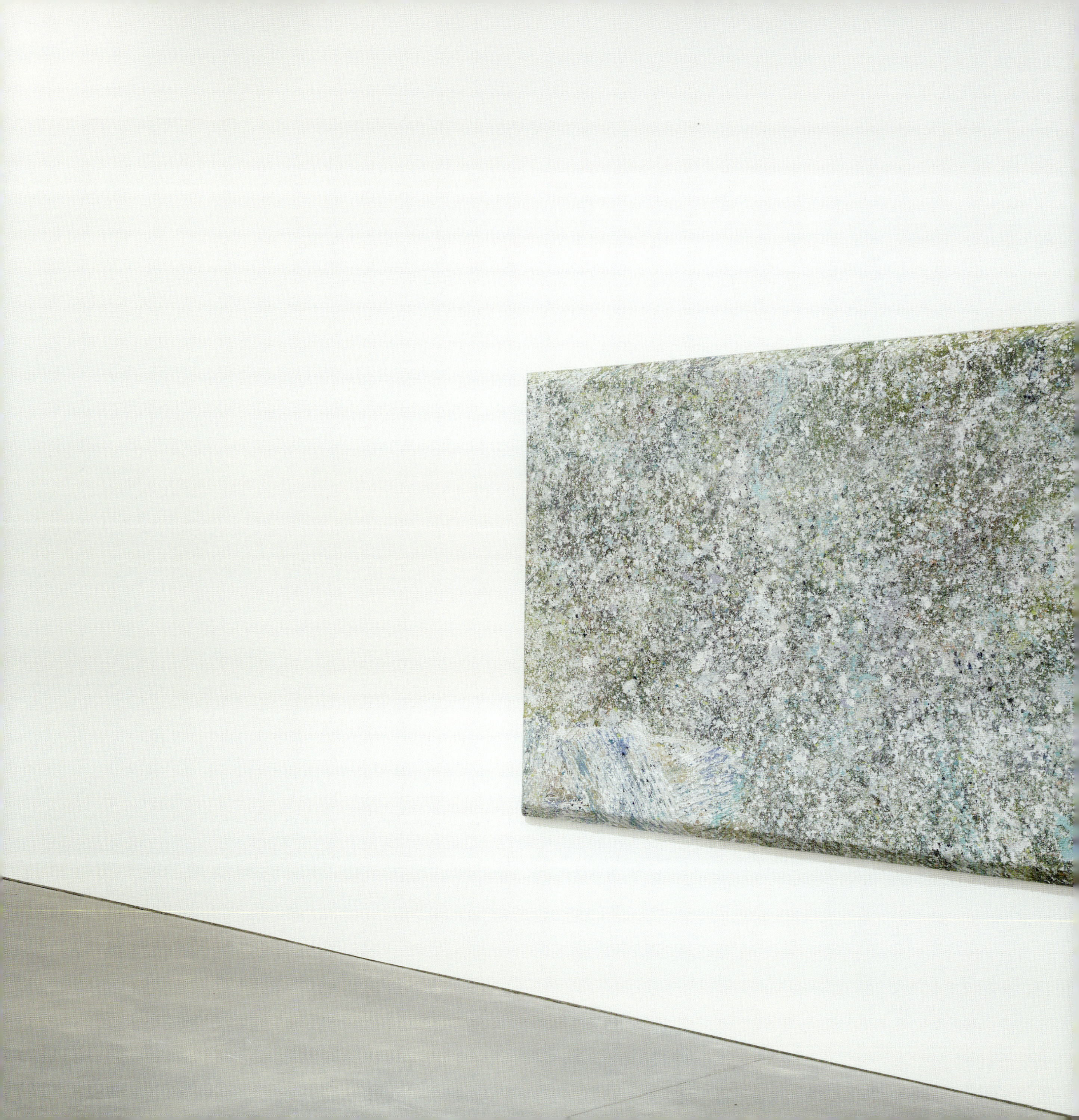

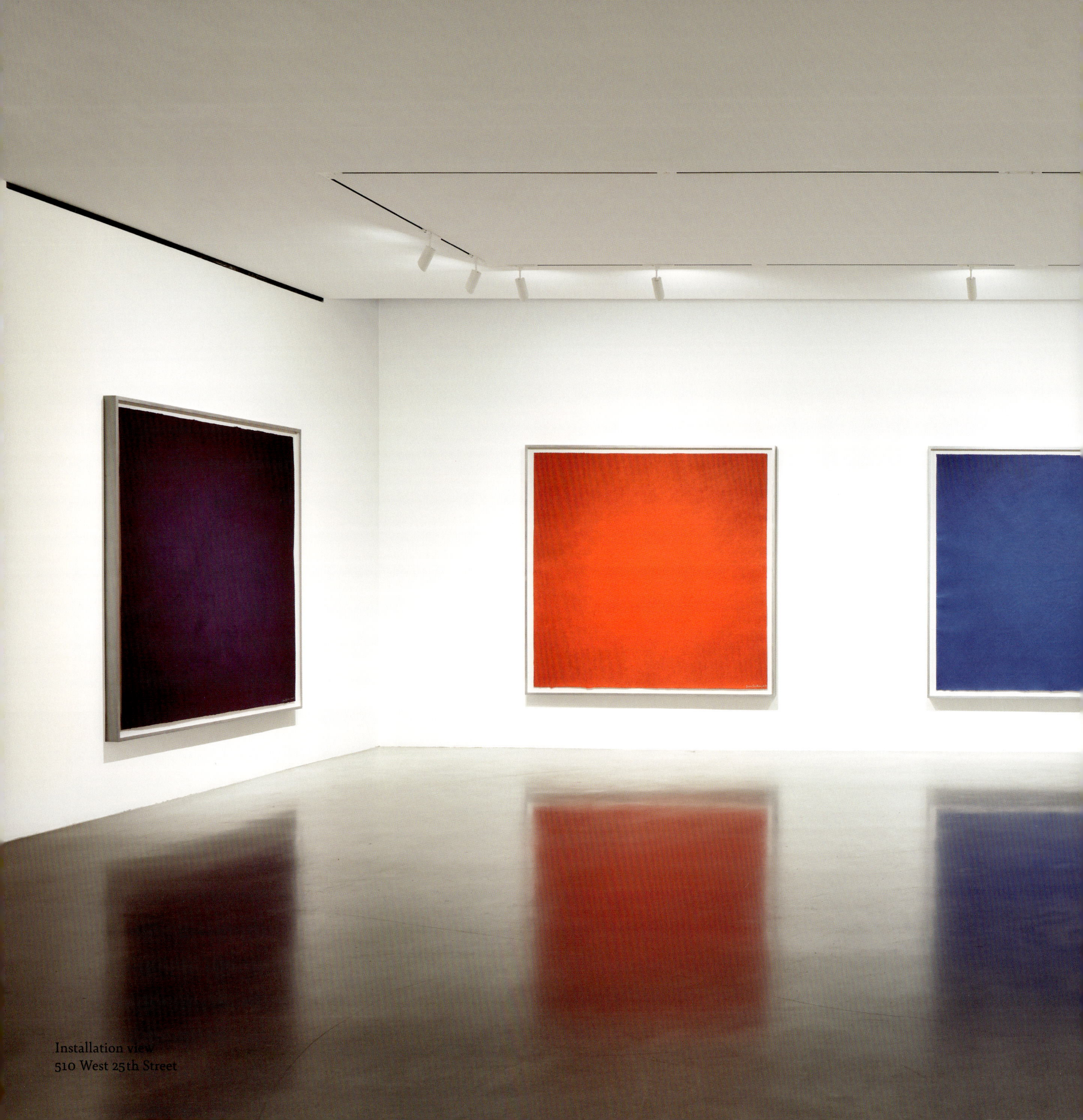

Installation view
510 West 25th Street

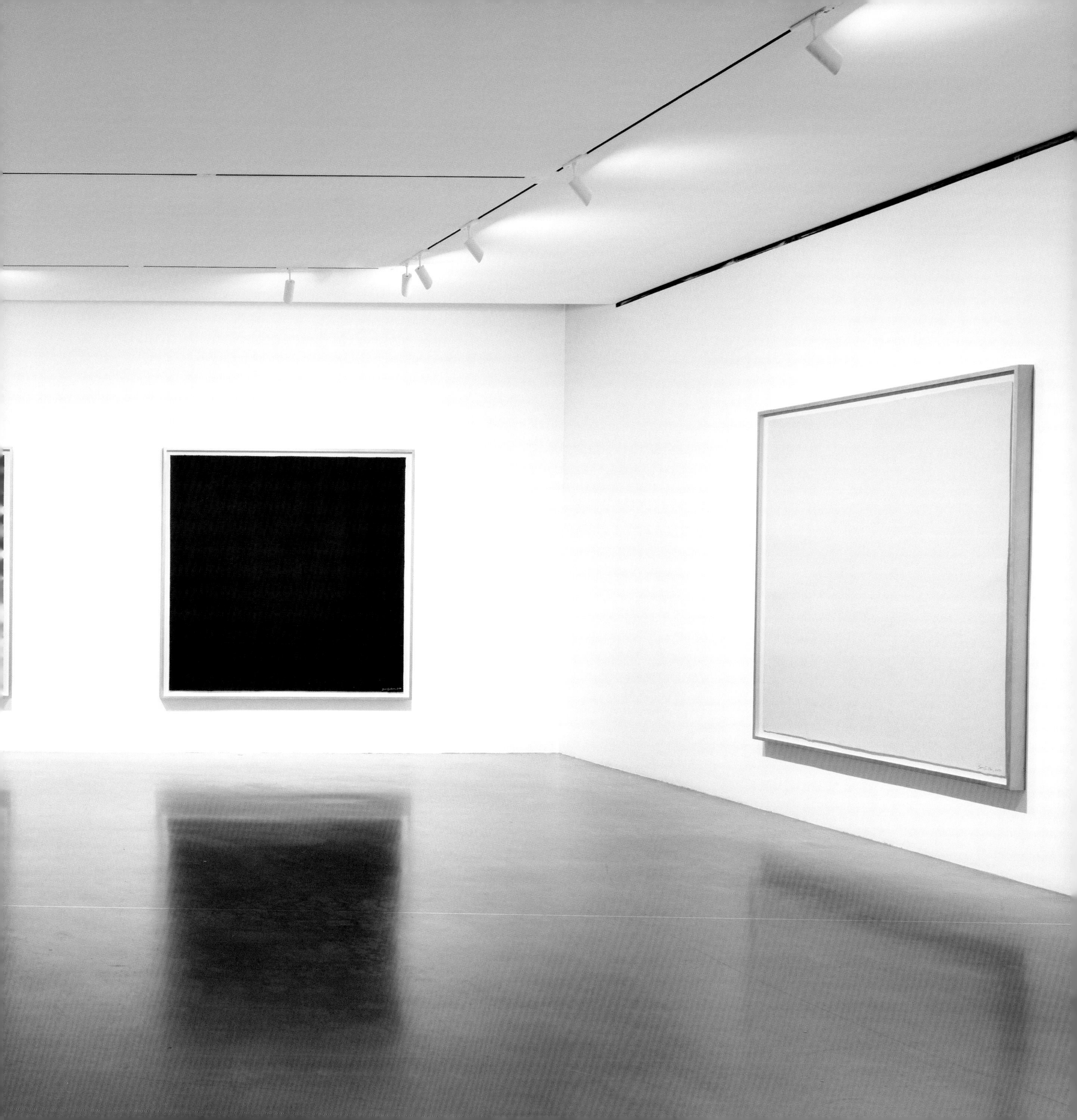

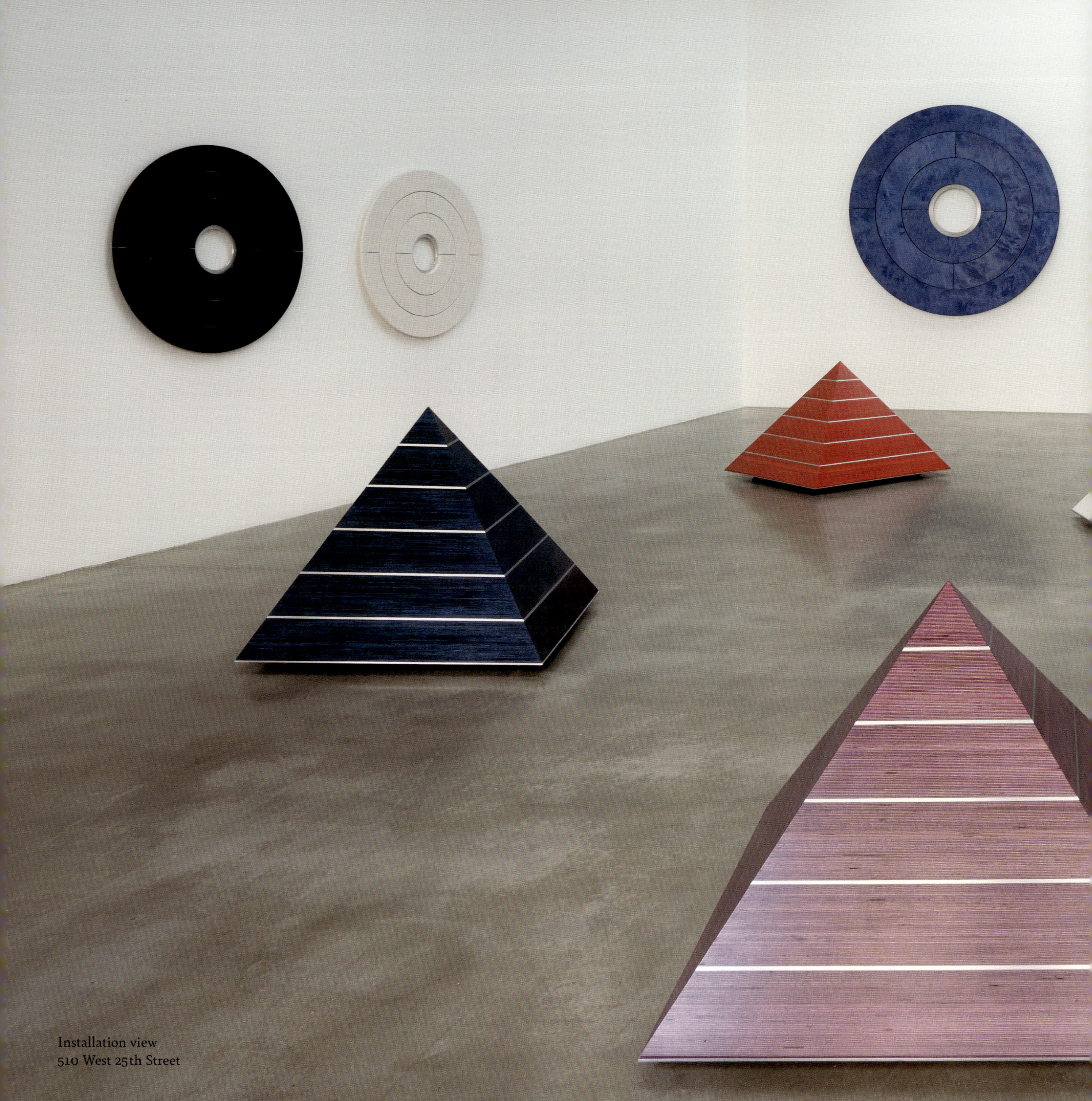

Installation view
510 West 25th Street

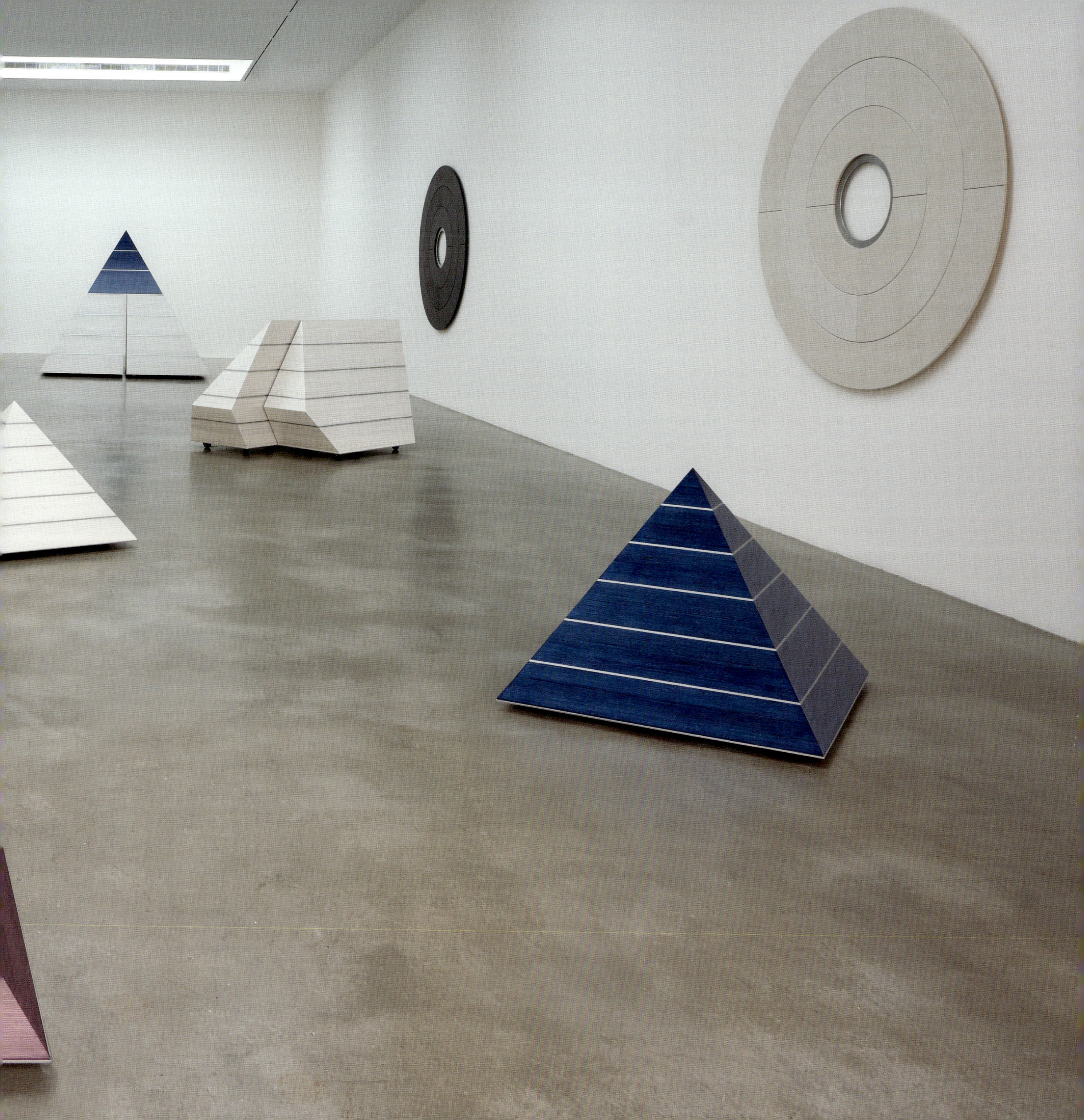

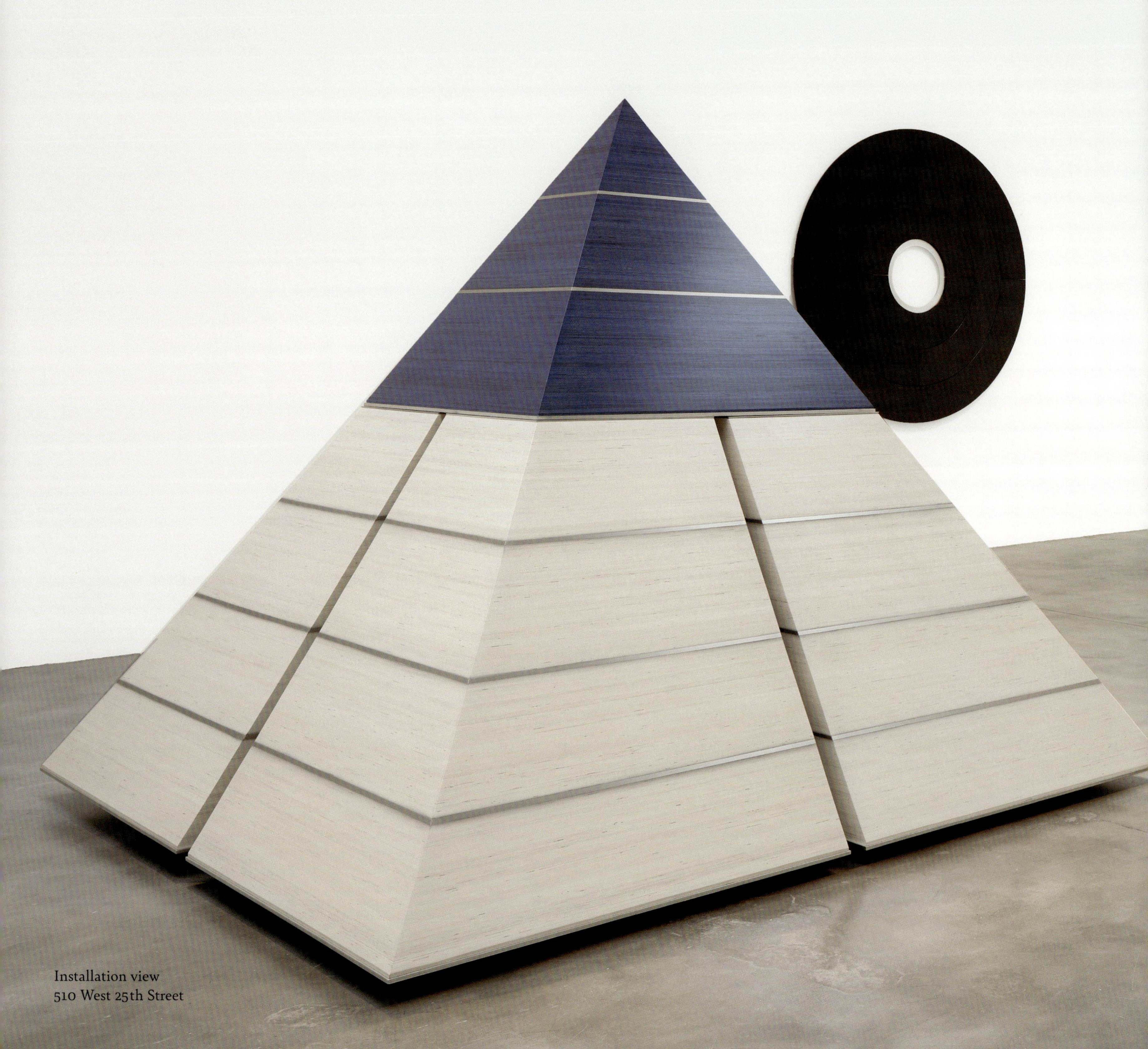

Installation view
510 West 25th Street

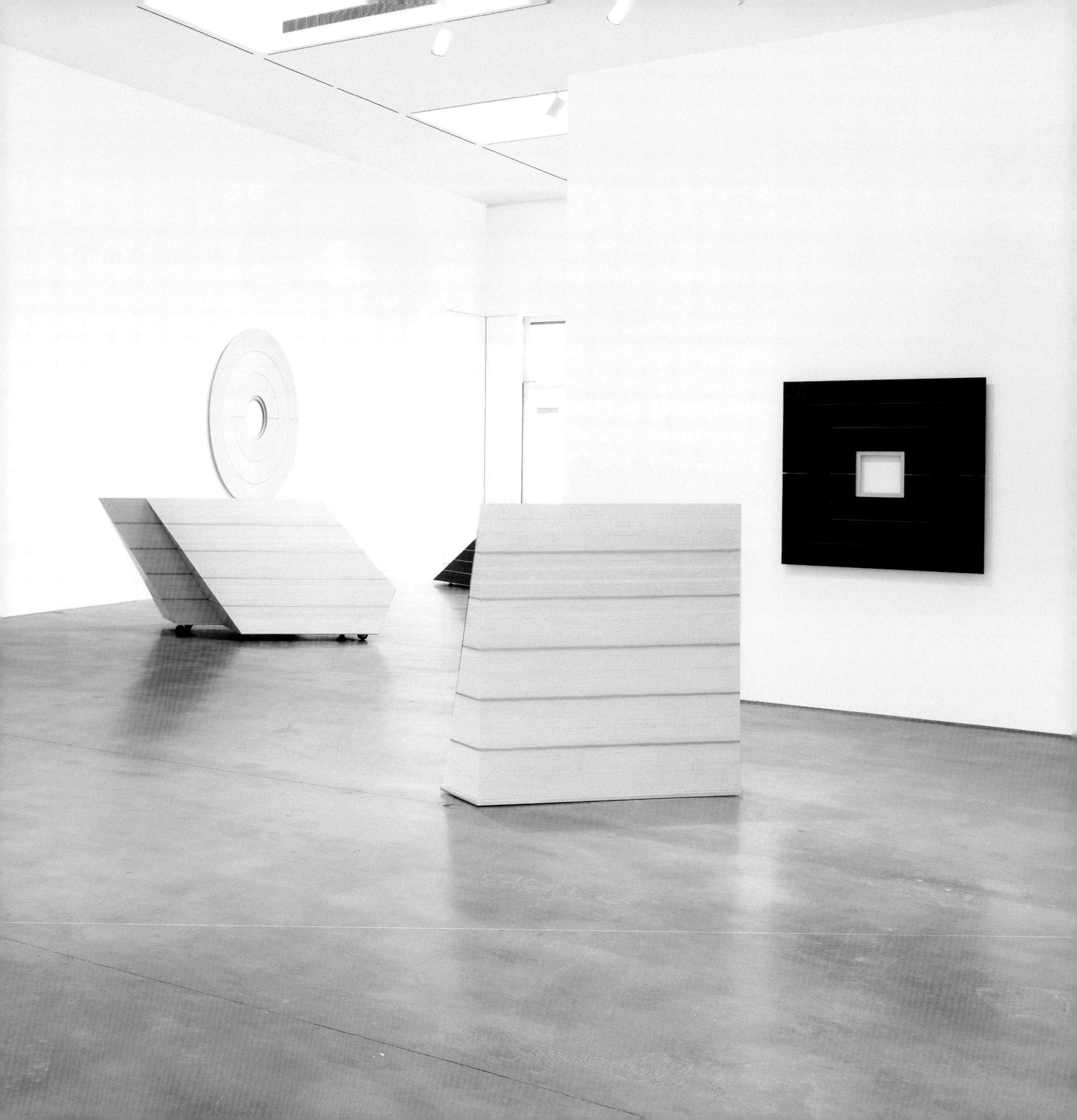

PAINTINGS

10–11 For John Lewis | 2020 | acrylic on canvas, 72 × 96 × 3 ¾"

12–13 Any Minute Now | 2020 | acrylic on canvas, 96 × 96 × 3 ¾"

14–15 A New Generation | 2020 | acrylic on canvas, 72 × 96 × 3 ¾"

16–19 October 18 | 2020 | acrylic on canvas, 8' × 20' × 3 ¾"

20–21 Heroines, Beyoncé, Serena and Althea | 2020 | acrylic on canvas, 72 × 96 × 3 ¾"

22–23 Waiting for "Dutchman" | 2020 | acrylic on canvas, 96 × 96 × 3 ¾"

26–27 The Mississippi "Shake Rag" | 2020 | acrylic on canvas, 96 × 96 × 4 ¾"

28–29 Purple Orpheus | 2020 | acrylic on canvas, 72 × 96 × 3 ¾"

30–31 Nikki Giovanni | 2020 | acrylic on canvas, 96 × 96 × 3 ¾"

32–35 They Dance and Sail Away | 2020 | acrylic on canvas, 8' × 20' × 3 ¾"

WASHI PAPERS

62–63 Washi Paper – Yellow | 2020 | acrylic on washi, 79 × 79"

64–65 Washi Paper – Purple/Black | 2020 | acrylic on washi, 79 × 79"

66–67 Washi Paper – Red | 2020 | acrylic on washi, 79 × 79"

70 Washi Paper – Turquoise | 2020 | acrylic on washi, 38 ⅝ × 38 ⅝"

71 Washi Paper – Blue V | 2020 | acrylic on washi, 38 ⅝ × 38 ⅝"

72–73 Washi Paper – Orange | 2020 | acrylic on washi, 79 × 79"

74–75 Washi Paper – Blue | 2020 | acrylic on washi, 79 × 79"

76–77 Washi Paper – Purple | 2020 | acrylic on washi, 79 × 79"

SCULPTURAL WORKS I

102–103 Blue 96" Disc | 2020 | wood, aluminum, die-stain, lacquer, 96 × 96 × 2 ¼"

104–105 Black 60" Disc | 2020 | wood, aluminum, die-stain, lacquer, 60 × 60 × 2 ¼" | variant 1 of 3

106–107 White 96" Disc | 2020 | wood, aluminum, die-stain, lacquer, 96 × 96 × 2 ¼"

108–109 Black Mozart/ ORNETTE | 2020 | wood, aluminum, die-stain, lacquer, 96 × 96 × 2 ¼"

110–111 White 48" Disc | 2020 | wood, aluminum, die-stain, lacquer, 48 × 48 × 2 ¼" | variant 1 of 4

112–113 Black 48" Square | 2020 | wood, aluminum, die-stain, lacquer, 48 × 48 × 2 ¼" | variant 1 of 8

SCULPTURAL WORKS II

126–133 Five Pyramids | 2020 | wood, aluminum, die-stain, lacquer, 36 ¼ × 48 × 48" each, 5 total
overall dimensions variable

136–137 Three White Pyramids | 2020 | wood, aluminum, die-stain, lacquer, 36 ¼ × 48 × 48" each, 3 total
overall dimensions variable | variants 2, 3, and 4 of 5

138–139 Pyramid | 2020 | wood, aluminum, die-stain, lacquer, 110 × 122 × 122"

140–141 Mastaba (In Two Parts) | 2020 | wood, aluminum, die-stain, lacquer, 54 × 114 × 61"

142 White Abacus | 2020 | wood, aluminum, die-stain, lacquer, 12 × 22 × 5" | variant 1 of 4

143 Color Abacus | 2020 | wood, aluminum, die-stain, lacquer, 12 × 22 × 5" | variant 1 of 4

Second printing

Front cover: *Blue 96" Disc* (detail), 2020
Endpaper (front): *Washi Paper – Yellow* (detail), 2020
Endpaper (back): *Washi Paper – Red* (detail), 2020

Photography:
Bridgeman Images: p. 120
Cathy Carver, Hirshhorn Museum and Sculpture Garden: p. 50
Courtesy the artist's studio: pp. 4, 36
Stephen Frietch, courtesy of David Kordansky Gallery, Los Angeles: p. 40
Art Frisch, courtesy San Francisco Chronicle/Polaris: p. 114
Melissa Goodwin: cover, endpapers, pp. 60–61, 63, 65, 67–71, 73, 75, 77–78, 98–99, 100–101, 103–105, 107, 109–111, 128–133, 135
Melissa Goodwin and Robyn Lehr Caspare: pp. 113, 142–143
Thierry Grun/Alamy Stock Photo: p. 94
Mark Gulezian/QuickSilver: p. 87
Phoebe d'Heurle: pp. 32–35
Phoebe d'Heurle & Christine Ann Jones: pp. 16–19, 126, 127, 137–139, 141, 146–155
Bill Jacobson Studio, New York, courtesy Dia Art Foundation: pp. 92–93
Bill Jacobson Studio, New York, courtesy The Greenwich Collection, Ltd.: p. 118
Johansen Krause, courtesy of the artist, the Philadelphia Museum of Art, Library & Archives, and David Kordansky, Los Angeles: p. 54
Maxwell Lee-Russell: p. 43
Nina Leen/The LIFE Picture Collection via Getty Images: p. 81
Erich Lessing/Art Resource, NY: p. 121
© The Metropolitan Museum of Art. Image source: Art Resource, NY: p.44
Courtesy of Mitchell-Innes & Nash, New York: p. 84; fig. 4
© The Museum of Modern Art/Licensed by SCALA/Art Resource, NY/Photograph by Michael Moran: p. 122
Jonathan Nesteruk: pp. 8–9, 11, 13, 15, 21, 23–25, 27, 29, 31, 84; fig. 3
Fredrik Nilsen Studio: p. 2
Fredrik Nilsen Studio, courtesy of David Kordansky Gallery, Los Angeles: p. 46
Smithsonian American Art Museum, Washington, DC/Art Resource, NY: p. 85; fig. 6
© Tate: p. 85; fig. 5
Lee Thompson, courtesy of Kunstmuseum Basel and David Kordansky Gallery, Los Angeles: p. 56

Design: Tomo Makiura & Mine Suda
Production: Pace Gallery
Color correction: Meridian Printing & Tucker Capparell
Copyediting: Sarah Stephenson
Printing: Meridian Printing, East Greenwich, Rhode Island

Typeset in Acumin Pro & Bely by Mine Suda

Library of Congress Control Number: 2020921882
ISBN: 978-1-948701-38-9